Men
Who
Build
Churches

Men Who Build Churches

Interpretations of the Life of Paul

Harold A. Bosley

ABINGDON PRESS

nashville and new york

MEN WHO BUILD CHURCHES

Copyright © 1972 by Abingdon Press

Library of Congress Cataloging in Publication Data

BOSLEY, HAROLD AUGUSTUS, 1907- . Men Who
Build Churches. 1. Paul, Saint, Apostle—Sermons.
2. Methodist Church—Sermons. 3. Sermons,
American. I. Title.
BS2506.B65   252'.07   72-701

ISBN 0-687-24801-9

MANUFACTURED BY THE PARTHENON PRESS AT
NASHVILLE, TENNESSEE, UNITED STATES OF AMERICA

To

BUILDERS OF CHURCHES
TODAY—AND TOMORROW

Students in my classes at
Crozer Theological Seminary
Westminster Theological Seminary
Duke Divinity School
Garrett Biblical Institute
New York Theological Seminary
Drew Theological Seminary

Foreword

"Why another book on Paul? Can anything new be said about him after all these years?" a close friend asked when he heard that this book was "in the works." Not being a devotee of the cult of novelty myself, I was not much moved by the second part of the inquiry, but the first part set me to thinking.

The very title of this book suggests the real answer to the question—*Men Who Build Churches.*

Paul was a churchman, i.e., he led men to Christ-in-community. He found and felt the presence of the Holy Spirit in the fellowship Christians had with one another. This awareness of uniqueness due to the activity of the Spirit led many early Christians to think of themselves as the "third race," related to but different from Jew and Gentile. Paul in his long ministry sought, through visits and letters, to guide and strengthen local congregations of Christians—especially the ones he had helped found. It is a lesson in wise, dedicated, human, and pragmatic churchmanship to see him at work with the problems of his people. One cannot read the several letters to the church in Corinth without sensing both his wisdom and impatience with the little issues that were troubling them. I suspect that every church leader—ancient and modern—has been driven up the wall repeatedly by the "little things" that annoy, aggravate, and sometimes divide a congregation. Paul worked with more than ordinary patience with his people, trying to keep their eyes on the great things, the ultimate goals, and aware of the warm presence of the Holy Spirit in their common life. His success in launching and nourishing churches depended upon his ability to do just this. He knew that the real bedrock of a church is the vital personal faith of the builders.

Church builder, yes—but not locked in some form of liturgy (good order, was all he asked!) or a special building (synagogue, civil court, jail, riverbank, rented hall—any and all provided a place to preach the gospel, which was all that really mattered). Paul combined in an unusual way dedication to the Christian fellowship with flexibility as to what form it should take. That, I suspect, is why he has been involved as one primary cause in nearly every new development in the history of Western Christendom. Augustine, one of the architects of the Catholic Church, tells how Romans 13:13 both brought his life under judgment and threw open the door to a new life. Luther was haunted by the word "the just shall live by faith" until he saw in it the true foundation for a church. Wesley was grasping for a new understanding of the meaning of faith when, at Aldersgate, Paul reached him through his despair and his heart was "strangely warmed." Karl Barth was completely changed both as theologian and person by his early studies in Paul's letters.

Paul was a preacher—a fact that should encourage us in a day when preaching is downgraded in many quarters of the church (usually by those who have never tried to learn the discipline of it). Teacher, debater—Paul was these too; but his cry "Woe is me if I preach not the Gospel" is the key to the heart of his life and work. It was fashioned in the agony of one who had to preach, even though he was dismayed by the results of it. The harder he preached, the more certain it was that mobs would form, stones would fly, and the police would drag everyone before some magistrate or other. Despite all this, Paul remained a preacher of the gospel to the end. He would preach any time, any place, any where and to any one who would listen. Given a chance to defend himself before Agrippa, he preached a sermon that wound up with a call to conversion!

Paul was no actor whose theatrical flare was better suited to the stage than the pulpit; he was a preacher in dead earnest about his message. He not only preached; he preached for a decision for Jesus Christ—an omission that weakens so much of our preaching today.

There is no way I can adequately express my gratitude to the many scholars who have slaved over the many facets of Paul's letters. Adolph Deissmann's *Paul*—now available in a paperback edition—opened up Paul's life, letters, faith and world in a memorable way. I am glad my understanding of Paul came under its influence early in my ministry. Excellent commentaries and translations keep coming from the presses of Christendom—and all are useful to one who would interpret Christ. The study of Paul seems to be waxing, not waning, today—a good omen for the future of the church. But one who wants to share in it must be prepared to invest big chunks of time, for Paul's letters, even the shortest of them, are not easy reading. Yet they offer us one of the greatest privileges of life—a walk with a truly "God-intoxicated man"—one who found the meaning of his life and work in the word of God spoken in Jesus Christ.

Over nearly half a century of preaching, I have found myself leaning more heavily on Paul than on any other biblical writer. While I have tried to keep faith with the Word of

God as it is found throughout the Bible, I have, nonetheless, kept coming back to Paul as the inspired guide to one, like myself, who is cast in the "leadership" role in a local church.

I trust that most women will not take offense at the title of the book. *Men* and *he* as I am using the terms, unless coupled with a definite masculine noun, are generic terms— as *Adam* is in Genesis. This book is based on Paul—and, to the best of my information, he was a man. As a local pastor for many years, I well know of the church's indebtedness to women as builders of churches.

The chapters in this book are but an earnest of the many efforts I have made over the years to relate Paul to our time. Some were sparked by a phrase or sentence; others by an event; others by a letter itself. Some—those of more formal style—were preached in seminaries and ministerial groups, but all were shared with the people committed to my care in Christ Church United Methodist of New York City to whom I shall be forever grateful.

HAROLD A. BOSLEY

Contents

1/Men Who Build Churches

Scripture: *Acts 22:1-22*

I

The quickest way to the human heart of a religious tradition is to study the various men and women who, through the centuries, have contributed so greatly to the building of it. While many deserve to be studied, there are a few whose influence proved to be a kind of historical watershed for the Christian movement. Paul, Augustine, Luther, Wesley are among those whose names loom large. Though separated by the centuries, they have much in common, especially this: all were devoted servants of Jesus Christ; all accepted him as their personal savior; all felt called to a life of service in the building of the kingdom of God through the Christian church. Living as we do in a day when the church is reported to be "losing her influence" in our common life, it is a tonic to dip into periods when the church was in even more difficult circumstances. Or into a period when there was no church at all, and men like Paul were trying to get one under way.

We cannot think of the early Christian church without thinking of Paul. His influence in the development of our tradition is second only to that of Jesus Christ. I am anxious that we meet him as a human being, a person. This will accentuate, not diminish, his greatness. I have no interest in the cheap kind of chumminess which our generation seems to require of its heroes, but I do want us to know him as a friend of all.

It comes as a shock to those of us who are accustomed to think of the greatness of Paul to realize that no contemporary historian mentions him. He had been dead a long time before he became a person of historical importance. But the materials out of which we construct our knowledge of him were very much a part of the early Christian community even though they and these communities were largely ignored by the court historians of the Caesars. Actually, we possess an amazing amount of information about Paul. Next to Jesus Christ, the New Testament tells us more about him than anyone else. And as we read it, we realize that Paul is the architect *par excellence* of the early church. No other man left so heavy, so definite, so creative an impression upon its thought and life as did he.

Paul wrote more of the New Testament than any other writer—about one-fourth of it—and the mark of his influence is clearly seen in much of the rest of it. His letters are the earliest documents in the New Testament to reach their present form. I never open his Letter to the Galatians without thinking: "This is the first book in the New Testament." Long before Matthew, Mark, Luke, and John were in existence, Paul's letters were circulated among Christian groups in the Mediterranean world. The Gospel of Mark, probably written in Rome, reached its form after Paul's ministry and death there. Matthew may have been written in whole or in part in Antioch some twenty-five years after Paul had begun his missionary activity there. Luke was written by one of Paul's intimate companions on one or more missionary journeys. John, written long after Paul's death, shows many

14

important evidences of his influence. And so it goes throughout most of the New Testament.

So we are not dismayed because Paul was overlooked by the historians of Greece and Rome. We know now that they must have missed a good many important people in that day, not least among whom were Jesus Christ and Paul.

Our knowledge of Paul's life and mind comes to us from his own letters. There is an interesting comparison between this and our way of knowing Emily Dickinson, a nineteenth-century American poet. Carl Van Doren tells us that it was not until after her death in 1886 "that even her family and friends know or even suspect that she had written the hundreds of poems which are found among her papers. She had spent most of the years of her life in an intense and increasing seclusion in the house in Amherst, Massachusetts, where she was born and where she died." "In her later years, she . . . seldom left her house and garden, and considered it an adventure to go through the hedge to her brother's house next door." Any objective historian of the town or times would have passed her by without comment—until her poems came to light! What poems! They range the world; they face unafraid the issues of life, love, and death; they give us an almost perfect expression of one of the most sensitive, courageous, and truthful spirits ever to live. Once men read her poems, they redrafted the history of Amherst, of American letters—giving Emily Dickinson the place she deserves.

Paul's letters have served in similar way though on a much broader and more important scale. There the similarity between Paul and Emily Dickinson ends. She was a recluse; he a tireless traveler. She was content to stay in her father's garden; he died having criss-crossed the Roman world several times—and planning to go to Spain. She lived and died within the culture pattern of her fathers; he broke with his with an explosion that rocked his life. She shied away from relationships with others; he laid foundations for Christian thought and the Christian church, cosmopolitan and universal in scope.

As we turn to his letters—so aptly described by Harris Franklin Rall as "conversations with his friends"—what sort of person do we discover? Certain important biographical facts emerge at once.

His life falls into three general periods. *First,* the Jewish period, which extends from his birth in A.D. 1 until he was about thirty-five years of age. *Then* come the three years of adjustment from thirty-five to thirty-eight, when, unhappily, he was outcast and hunted by the Jews on the one hand, and not yet accepted by the Christians, on the other. *The third period* extends from his thirty-eighth year to the end of his life at sixty-four—covering twenty-six years. It sees him forging to the foreground as a great Christian thinker and leader. A glance at each of these periods covered in his letters will throw light on a man building a church.

II

Paul was born and spent the largest part of his life in Tarsus, a city in Asia Minor. Tarsus, as he tells us, was "no mean city"; in fact, it was one of the most important cities in the eastern Mediterranean area. It was the home of the Roman Governor of that province. It boasted of one of the three great universities of the time, the others being at Athens and Alexandria. It was a thriving center of travel and commerce. A student of Paul's life has written of it,

"The Cilician plain on which Paul lived as boy and man has, from the most ancient time, been a center of international intercourse." Paul's homeland has always been "the threshold of two civilizations and the bridge between two worlds."

His parents were devout Jews, and their son was brought up to love the synagogue, to revere the Law, and to look forward to the day when he could go to the Holy City, tread the sacred precincts of the Temple and, perchance, study with the great teachers there. Paul's father possessed and passed on to him the unusual distinction of being a full-fledged Roman citizen—which meant that Paul, by birth, was a Roman citizen. His parents, like all good Jews, taught their son a trade—tent making—and sent him to Jerusalem to study when he was about thirty-three years of age, perhaps hoping he would become a Rabbi.

Paul was a religious volcano—there is no other way to describe him—as he headed for Jerusalem. The intensity and sincerity of his loyalty to his beliefs all through his life made him as intolerant a person as we are likely ever to meet. He was a partisan—an intense partisan—never a spectator, in the disputes that raged in Jerusalem. To believe something meant to fight for it and to try to destroy whoever challenged it. He regarded the Jews who had embraced Christianity as traitors to their people and destroyers of the Law. Hence, he became the leader of one of the mobs of Zealots who were out to destroy the Christian sect. While many tolerant Jewish leaders in Jerusalem must have viewed his activities with dismay, some encouraged him. He and his gang killed Stephen by stoning, and drove various Christian groups in Jerusalem underground. Not satisfied with his victory there, he set out for Damascus with permission to carry on his anti-Christian crusade. And it was on the road to

Damascus that both the course of his life and the course of history were profoundly altered.

III

The New Testament gives us three separate and, in minor ways, different versions of what happened on the Damascus Road. Psychologists are at liberty to do what they can with the facts at hand—and the facts are too few for a good case study—but historians simply record the fact that Paul became a Christian, a member of the sect he had been persecuting so savagely. Where once he had rejected as blasphemous the claim that Jesus was the Messiah, he now accepted it. Where once he had sought to scatter and destroy the Christian sect, he now became one of its greatest leaders. The basic belief of his life was that God had called him to make the change; that it was God who had appointed him to preach the gospel to all who would listen.

It was a hard transition, both for him to make and for those who knew him to accept. He did not make it easily or without severe struggle. And we should find it easy to understand the hatred which "the Jews" showered upon him, once he had made the change. No one likes a traitor, a turncoat, or a renegade—as his erstwhile friends and supporters regarded him. They tried to kill him—not once, but many times.

Nor is it difficult to understand the Christians' hesitation over accepting him in their group. We cannot read the story of his initial reception in Damascus immediately after his conversion without feeling that the Christians there, despite his claim to be one of them, breathed easier when they got rid of him.

Paul spent at least three wretched years—maybe more— here, there, and yonder ("in the desert" he said), trying to get his life reorganized after this explosion. The old pattern was gone. What had once seemed so firm lay in pieces all around him. He was a new man in a new world—and, at first, it must have been a frightening experience. It took awhile for him to get his life reorganized around his new convictions and loyalties. Then the miracle of faith occurred. As he stirred the ashes of his old faith, the flames of a new one burst out! He became as intense a Christian as he had been a Jew. Consequently, he was ready and willing to enter into the life of the church in Antioch when opportunity offered. And, in doing so, the third and greatest period of his life began.

IV

He began his career as a Christian missionary in a quiet way and under the guidance of Barnabas. Christian leaders, knowing that the Jews of Palestine would harass, if not kill him, should he return there, directed his efforts north and west, "to the Gentiles," as he put it.

Off he went on his missionary journeys, sometimes with Barnabas, sometimes Silas, sometimes Luke as his companions.

Recently, a contemporary student of Paul's life went over the routes of his three missionary journeys as nearly as we are able to construct them. He reflects, "One of the most lasting impressions of these journeys, made for the most part with all modern conveniences for travel, is inexpressible astonishment at the purely physical achievement of Paul the traveller." He was on the move the last twenty-six years of his life, preaching the gospel wherever he went. His longest stop seems to have been in Ephesus—another great city—where he stayed, teaching and preaching nearly three years. Name any great seacoast city in the eastern Mediterranean, and Paul was there. Twenty-six years without a home of his own—that's the story of the last period of his life. His home, if you can call it that, was where he was preaching. He plied his trade, supporting himself wherever he went. For the most part, the little groups of Christians among whom he worked were too poor to do much toward the support of traveling evangelists, though they did send gifts to Paul when he was in prison and to other Christian groups that were in greater need than their own.

When Paul went to a community, he went to the synagogue first and tried to persuade the Jews that Jesus was the Messiah. He failed to convince many—and, frequently, was thrown out bodily for having tried it. Then he would preach on street corners, in public parks, or wherever he could get a group together. If there were a Christian group in the community, he would work and live with them. Almost all his letters abound with warm personal greetings to such friends wherever he had been.

Paul met with limited but important success. He left an inerasable impression on every group he touched. They treasured his letters and passed them on to their children as precious documents. He is, and remains to this day, "the great missionary" of our tradition.

But Paul had his troubles. He was hounded by critics all his life. Loyal Jews, Jewish-Christians, Gentiles—all furnished their quota of critics of Paul. And we might as well admit the plain fact that he had all too little patience with them. His critics accused him of nearly everything in the book: of lying, stealing, of deceiving his listeners about his right to preach, and of being too harsh with the brethren. If a man is going to get mad about anything, he will certainly get mad about charges like these, I suppose. Well, Paul got mad—that's as plain as day. His wrath played like summer lightning about them, especially in the letter to the Galatians and sections of II Corinthians. He turned on one group of detractors and hoped they would be emasculated. He turned on another and readily consigned them to hell. It is amazing how much freedom of expression I feel as I read Paul and seek to be guided by him! No one, reading his letters, would ever be inclined to sing of him as we do of Jesus: "Gentle Paul, meek and mild." He was a religious volcano to the end of his life, and the lava of his wrath poured out on all sides when he erupted.

Paul could be wrong, too. And he admitted it. He thought young John Mark had deliberately deserted the missionary team on the first journey that he took with Barnabas and others. That did it for Mark, so far as Paul was concerned. No more journeys with him. Barnabas thought differently; he wanted to give Mark another chance. That did it for Barnabas! No more journeys with Barnabas!

How, when, and why Paul changed his mind about Mark, we do not know, but we do know that years later in a note urging Timothy to come to see him when he was in prison. he adds: "Take Mark, and bring him with thee: for he is profitable to me for the ministry."

There is comfort for me and warning for you in the fact that his sermons were not always interesting! Upon at least one occasion, a young man named Eutychus went to sleep during one of Paul's sermons and fell out of the window in which he was sitting and broke his neck. There is more comfort for me than warning for you in that incident, though, because it is exceedingly difficult to sit in modern church windows, let alone go to sleep there! And there is no need for it. Our pews are quite comfortable.

The last glimpse of Paul furnished by the New Testament shows him at Rome, waiting for the hearing he has requested before Caesar. He is under house arrest and able to visit with and preach to whoever comes to see him.

A later tradition tells us that he was condemned to death and killed in one of the waves of persecution that began to sweep over the Christian group. Novelists from Sienkiewicz to Sholem Asch have rushed in to fill the gap with their imagination, but we have little or no reliable information about the actual end of Paul's life on this earth.

But, however it may have ended physically, it lived— and lives on—gloriously in the life and work of the Christian church. For he, truly, was a builder of churches.

V

There is no explaining or summing up a life like that! It's so much of a piece that we take it or leave it whole.

Looking at the whole of his life as we see it in the New Testament, I am impressed by his ability to keep such sharp contrasts in one personality. As a great German student of his life has said, "[He] had room in his personality for contradictions which would have hopelessly shattered a small man . . . but [they] did not shatter Paul; they gave his inner life that tremendous tension which expressed itself in the energy put forth in his life-work."

On the one hand, he was humble—as humble a man as we know, yet self-confident to the point of being self-righteous.

He was humble before God, and in the presence of Jesus Christ he could not so much as lift up his head. He was mindful of his indebtedness to many men, both Jew and Gentile, yet he was sure of his gospel, sure of his call to take the gospel to the Gentiles—and woe betide whoever questioned either!

Paul was "tender, yet intolerant." He never forgot his people's need. His letters radiate concern, compassion, sympathy, and understanding. He had been such a sinner himself that he found it easy to understand sinners. He had gone through so much himself "for Christ's sake," that he understood the temptations and hardships of others who were trying to live the Christian life. Yet he demanded utmost and unswerving loyalty of his followers. He had as little patience with those who sought to block his path as with those who deserted him. Driving as he was, dead ahead at full speed, men were either with him or against him. Someone has said —perhaps truly—"There has probably seldom been anyone at the same time hated with such fiery hatred and loved with such strong passion as Paul."

Though his life was rocked from explosions, he was never driven to despair by them. He took them as from God—as God's way of saying, "No! You must leave the old and go on to something new!" As Paul picked up such pieces as he could carry and went ahead, he became a second Abraham. Fortunately for us, he knew how to live creatively with the explosions that shook his life.

Paul has stood the test of time. The hatreds have vanished, and only the high esteem, the admiration, the love, remain. We study his writings with zeal and respect. We name our children and our churches after him. We acknowledge him to be second only to Jesus Christ in our New Testament. We hail him as one of the greatest—if not the greatest—builder of churches in our tradition. But, above all, we say of him: "He was a man sent of God to work a mighty work in his own life, in the lives of his people, and in ours, as well."

2/They Write Letters with Purpose

Scripture: *II Corinthians 2:14–3:6*

I

When the mailman comes to our house, we rush to the door, asking, "Is there a letter for me?" As I receive mine, I wonder whether they bear a blessing or a curse!

But letters command our attention, and whether we like them or not, we read them.

Each letter may contain a mystery, but there is little mystery about what a letter is. A letter is a part of a written conversation between persons who share a common interest. Reading a letter that has been written to someone else is a little like hearing a person talking on the telephone. Though we hear only half of the conversation, we are able to construct with some accuracy the whole conversation. There are all kinds of letters because there are all kinds of people, all sorts of interests, all sorts of problems, and many degrees of sharing them with other people.

We see this in a dramatic way in a big volume brought out in 1940 under the title, *The World's Great Letters*. This book contains an infinite variety of the letters! The editor himself says, "Here are love letters, taunting letters, shocking letters, letters dipped in honeyed phrases, letters written with words of gall, bombastic letters, letters breathing fire, letters with good news, letters spelling disaster, passionate letters, secret letters, casual letters, gushing letters, impulsive letters, crafty letters, open letters, grandiloquent letters, short letters, voluminous letters, letters, of hatred, letters of courage, letters of adoration, letters of fury, letters people forgot to burn, letters people did not dare to mail, thundering letters, tender letters, inspired letters, diabolical letters, letters that made history."

I find it always interesting to read the letter reportedly written by Abraham Lincoln to Mrs. Lydia Bixby upon receipt of the news that she had lost five sons in the Civil War. I cannot grasp the apparent casualness of the letter Thomas Jefferson wrote on the very day that he addressed himself to the task of drafting the Declaration of Independence! And there are many other equally interesting letters that will live as long as men inhabit this planet and are interested in one anothers' lives. Letters are important loopholes on life: the life of the one who writes; the one to whom they are written; the situation that calls them into being.

There is an interesting difference between the Old and New Testaments on this matter of letters. The three or four genuine letters in the Old Testament are portions of larger books. One of the most interesting is Jeremiah's letter to the exiles in Babylon written in the seventh century. The editors of Jeremiah's prophecies found this letter and included it in the book which bears his name. When we read it, we are reading a document that is easily 2,500 years old, yet as fresh and alive today as it was then.

With a few exceptions like this, letters do not occur in the Old Testament. But in the New Testament the tables turn; letters loom large. In fact, all of the New Testament, with the exception of the Four Gospels and the Book of Acts, is in the form of letters. And there is room to argue the point that the Gospel of Luke is the first half, and the

Book of Acts the second half, of a long letter Luke was writing a friend who had asked for information about the Christian movement. The box score for the New Testament reads something like this: of its twenty-seven books, three are not letters, two may not be letters, and twenty-two are undoubtedly letters of one kind or another. Of these twenty-two, twelve are attributed to Paul, and the rest to other leaders of the early church.

This interesting fact opens the door on one characteristic of the early church: it was knit together both by traveling evangelists and by a literal flood of letters from one church to another; from one preacher or leader to the churches he had served; or from a leader who wanted to influence the life of a certain church in some way or other. This seems to have been the rule: if the one who had something to say to the churches could go in person and say it, he went; but if he were prevented from making the trip, he sent a letter by a personal friend.

While we have only a fragment of the voluminous correspondence that helped the scattered churches grow together, there is reason to believe that we have the letters that proved to be the most helpful and were the most widely treasured in the church.

II

Among the writers of letters that live, the name of Paul is without equal in the New Testament and, indeed, in our heritage. Beginning with the churches to whom they were written and spreading in ever-widening circles, his letters were known and respected in the early church. The earliest reference to them is in the New Testament itself, in II Peter:

"Therefore, beloved . . . be zealous to be found by [our Lord] without spot or blemish, and at peace. . . . So also our beloved brother Paul wrote to you according to the wisdom given him, speaking of this as he does in all his letters. There are some things in them hard to understand, which the ignorant and unstable twist to their own destruction as they do the other scriptures" (3:14-16 RSV).

During a persecution of Christians in the year 180, three traveling evangelists were arrested and brought before a Roman magistrate. The prosecutor charged that they had evil magic in the box they were carrying. They denied this, saying that in that box were "the books used by us, and besides these, the letters of the holy man, Paul."

Paul's letters have continued to live with power in subsequent generations. Augustine, living some 300 years after Paul, was led into the church by them, and from them he continued to draw inspiration and insight. When Luther was hammering out the outline of the Reformation, he used the conviction of Augustine and Paul—"The just shall live by faith." The insight that had served Paul so well against the legalism in Judaism served Luther in his struggle against the legalism in medieval Roman Catholicism.

We do but bring the story up to date to remember that when Karl Barth, in the 1920s, wanted to discover the power of the Christian faith, he found it in the letters of Paul—especially the one to the Romans.

These twelve letters that lie so quietly and live so undisturbed and undisturbing an existence in our Bibles today have been the seedbed of revival and renewal time after time over 2,000 years! What others in days of deep concern and need have found so luminous and helpful, children of the night in which we live cannot afford to ignore!

III

Letters like these tell us much about the man who wrote them and the people to whom they were written. We are, as it were, in the room with Paul as he is engaging in conversations with various people and churches. What he says and how he says it tell us something about him, the ones to whom he writes, and the life of the early church.

In fact, these letters, together with the Book of Acts, give us nearly all we know about the first half-century of the Christian church. But it is Paul—the writer, the author, the doubter, the thinker, the preacher—we see in the letters. One of the most powerful personalities ever to emerge in the history of man takes shape as we study them. Every letter contains its own picture of him. In them we discover not the premeditated polish of an essay by Bacon or Emerson, but "a natural blazing out of hidden greatness." They give us what might be called a composite picture of Paul—with each one illuminating a facet of his character and spirit. As we read them, a fairly precise picture of him and the ones to whom he writes takes shape.

He was a Jew, born in Tarsus, a city in Asia Minor. His father was a Roman citizen. He himself had inherited his Roman citizenship—and was proud of it, even when the Roman government put him to death as a subversive. He was raised in the synagogue and possibly trained for the rabbinate. In addition, he was taught the trade of tent-making. While in his thirties, he went to Jerusalem to complete his training for religious leadership. There, his zeal for the faith led him into persecuting the heretical sect later to be called Christians. He was converted to their belief that Jesus was the Messiah, and immediately became as zealous a Christian as he had been a Jew.

Disowned by his own people and suspected by the Christians for awhile, he felt called of Christ to turn his attention to the proclamation of the gospel in the Gentile world. Signal success marked his efforts and convinced him that Christ was the Savior of all men and should be taken to all men, and that God had called him to be the apostle to the Gentiles. Off he went on one long missionary journey after another to the very end of his life, founding churches wherever he went. He formed his converts into small groups and kept in touch with them by repeated trips, by sending traveling companions like Timothy to see how they were prospering, and, above all, by letters designed to answer their questions, to help them with their problems, to deepen their faith, and to guard them against false teachings. He dictated his letters to readily available scribes who might or might not be Christian. He wrote only a few lines in his own hand as postscripts. He spent all of his time teaching, preaching, and traveling by land and by sea to place after place which needed to hear the gospel.

Over twenty-five long, hard, fruitful years went into this—and, in the end, Paul was second only to Jesus as a power in the formation of the early church. Any effort to present Peter as a power equal—much less superior—to Paul is a simple misreading of every known fact about the two. Paul may not have been widely known outside the Christian church at that time, but he is the great missionary whose loving, tireless efforts planted the church firmly in one great city after another and whose brilliant mind plunged him to the heart of Christian truth and made it available to all men.

As we see Paul in his letters, we see one whose life is a

fascinating blend of strength and weakness, humility and confidence, tenderness and firmness. There is no gainsaying the fact that he was both loved and hated more completely than any other early leader. As Deissmann has said: "He did not know the comfortable quietness of the ordinary man. His way of life lay through the fire and tempest of love and hate." Sholem Asch caught this fact and made it central in his historical novel about Paul which he gave the eloquent title, *The Apostle*.

IV

If a letter is a part of a written conversation, it tells us something about both the writer and the reader. This is specially true of Paul's letters; they give us some interesting pictures of the communities for whom they were written. II Corinthians contains a reference to a letter of questions sent Paul by the Christians in Corinth. The questions were intensely practical in nature: Should a Christian who is married to a pagan get a divorce? Should a Christian buy meat at a market near a pagan shrine when the meat has been secured from sacrifices brought to the altar of that shrine? Should an unmarried Christian marry? Should Christians take cases to pagan courts for decision? How should Christian women dress and conduct themselves in church? What should be done to keep order in the public meetings of the Christian fellowship? How should Christians conduct a service commemorating the Last Supper of our Lord with his Disciples?

Paul attempts to answer these in his typical forthright way. But in question and answer we have, as one scholar suggests, the roof lifted off the church at Corinth and we can see what they do, hear what they say, and get some notion of who they are. If we expect to see wealthy or learned or powerful people among them, we shall be disappointed. None such came into the early church. A hundred and more years had to elapse before Christianity made any significant impression on this class of people.

The people in the early Christian groups were "common folk"—that much is clear on every page of the New Testament as well as in every other scrap of historical evidence we have.

Read again the straightforward way Paul reassures the Christians in Corinth. Apparently, they were flinching under the judgments of the sophisticated, cultured people there. Paul steadied them with these wise and gentle words, "For consider your call, brethren; not many of you were wise according to worldly standards, not many were powerful, not many were of noble birth; but God chose what is foolish in the world to shame the wise; . . . God chose what is low and despised in the world, even things that are not, to bring to nothing things that are, so that no human being might boast in the presence of God" (I Corinthians 1:26-29 RSV).

Words like these were reassuring, not alone to the Christians in Corinth in the first century, but to Christians generally for the next 250 years. For they were the target of abuse, scorn, harsh judgments, and persecution from every quarter of the Greco-Roman world. A pagan philosopher, Celsus by name, writing a hundred years after Paul's day, exclaims sarcastically that Christians are so immoral as to say, "Everyone . . . who is a sinner, who is devoid of understanding, who is a child, and . . . whoever is unfortunate, him will the Kingdom of God receive."

Nor is Celsus alone in this. In the nineteenth century,

Gibbon—bitterly contemplating the decline and fall of the Roman Empire—gives the Christians the back of his hand in this violent (if classic) judgment: "Christians were almost entirely composed of the dregs of the populace—of peasants and mechancis, of boys and women, of beggars and slaves." Probably the most reliable estimate from the historian is that of Shirley Jackson Case: "Christians were composed of the working class and small tradesmen; the majority were slaves, common laborers and people without recognized social status."

Any way, we look at it, no one joined the early Christian church for social or economic or political reasons; it made its way most rapidly in the lowest social stratum of that day. Yet, it could not be confined to that group. In the course of time it burst upward and outward with amazing rapidity.

Looking at Paul's letters, we are led to the conclusion that Christianity grew because it had the common touch. It gave men—*all* men, even the most lowly—a status before God that no human power could either give or take away. Hence, it came to be prized by kings and subjects, masters and slaves, rich and poor, alike. Using the language of ordinary people and addressing itself to the problems they felt important, the gospel could go wherever men were, could start a mission, and could interpret itself as light and power in the lives of men—and it did just that!

The early church quite literally and proudly proclaims *its commonness, its earthiness, its simplicity;* and in it we discover a new appreciation of the power—the sheer power —of ordinary people, ordinary language, and ordinary relationships. Perhaps we do this with a certain wistfulness today because we find it so easy for churches to lose the common

33

touch, that distinctive quality of the church in the days of her greatness.

V

There are several reasons why Paul's letters were treasured then, and continue to live today. Suppose we had been on the receiving end of these letters then. What would they have meant to us? We can't really say, can we? But we are on the receiving end of them now! They have become the common property of our religious heritage. They have something for us as truly as they had something for the ones who first received them. If we will read them as though Paul had written to us, we will discover several things about them, about Paul, and about ourselves.

We will say of the one who wrote them, "Here is a man of deep conviction. He has something to say, and he has earned the right to say it. He has suffered for it; he is honest about it; he is committed to it. He is concerned about the most important thing in the world: the right relationship of man with God. He has found it in Christ, and he wants others to find it there, too."

Paul's letters reveal the costliness of this discovery. He has had to leave all else behind: home, family, and hallowed religious tradition. But the discovery of God in Christ has been worth it all. It lays claim to his entire life. He is a slave of Christ, an ambassador of Christ, a steward of the mysteries of God—by his own confession.

Several letters relate his conversion experience—how Christ came to him, rebuking and forgiving him for his sins, and ordering him to take the gospel to the Gentiles. He recounts this, not only to validate his own ministry, but also to make the point that all Christians are called of God in Christ to preach the gospel.

Paul's letters contain expressions that are off-the-cuff, but his basic positions are carefully thought out. He does not rest his faith on a moment of emotional excitement. *He thinks it out; he thinks it through*—until it makes the kind of sense he can share with other people.

Read Paul's letters and we will say, "Here is a man who not only has convictions, but *he has the courage of those convictions.*" He finds in them courage enough to break with the past, including his family (there is no other way to interpret his complete silence on this); to turn away from his earlier training for service in Judaism. He finds in them courage to struggle with his Christian brethren for an understanding of the new faith that would open it to all men. He finds the courage to face the massive indifference of the rest of the world toward the gospel. For twenty-six years and over thousands of miles and in hundreds of places, he goes where the Spirit of God leads him.

Paul has more than the courage of his convictions: *he is insistent about them.* He insists upon communicating them to other people with an urgency that borders on impertinence. I seldom read these letters without recalling an unusually honest person who said of him, "Paul offends me by his exhortations. He is too insistent about it all."

If we are offended by intensity of conviction, we will surely take offense at him—and Augustine, and Martin Luther, and John Wesley, and Martin Luther King, and everyone else who insists upon declaring the relevance of his faith to the problems of the day in which he lives. Paul is insistent in his presentation of his convictions; he does exhort people constantly, refusing to give any man rest until he has made his peace with them. If we are uncomfortable around intense people, we will be uncomfortable around him and every other man who has served as a pivot in the development of our religious heritage.

Read Paul's letters and we will see a man who simply must share his convictions with anyone who will listen—and some who seem not to care. Not for a single moment does he flirt with the modern heresy that "my religion is my own affair; it is a purely personal matter; I can believe whatever I want to believe and so can you." Paul hammers away unceasingly at the point that we must be obedient to the word of God which we find in Jesus Christ. Christ is God's full and true word spoken to men who are willing to hear and to obey him. Hence, the importance of preaching. All men must hear the word, must know of Christ, must be confronted with his claim on them. All who believe in Jesus Christ must be preachers of the word wherever they are.

No matter how weak the flesh may be, Paul's spirit never flags. "Woe is me if I preach not the gospel!" is his own way of describing the powerful compulsion that drives him throughout his life as a Christian. We see both what Paul expects of himself and of all Christians in this mighty statement of faith and work: "God was in Christ, reconciling the world unto himself, . . . and hath committed unto us the word of reconciliation." Here, Paul wrote, is what we believe, and this is what we are supposed to do about it.

Letters like these live; they fascinate most people who really read them. It isn't hard to see why, is it? They are expressions of a great faith: a faith on which a man stakes his life; a faith that is incandescent with a divine power and purpose that brings light into the darkness of all who will accept it; a faith that proves to be a contagious center of new loyalty over thousands of years.

Living as we do in a day when we hunger for faith—when we are tired of trying to warm our hands and our hearts over the cold ashes of the little fires once kindled by our conceits about what man could do—we need to know men like Paul, need to feel the power of his faith, need to wait in obedient spirit for a call to us from the One who called Paul and gave him work fit for one who was prepared to share in the work of the God who made him. Then we will become what Paul held before the Corinthians as an ideal: Living Epistles—"The epistle of Christ . . . written not with ink, but with the Spirit of the living God; not in tables of stone, but in the fleshy tables of the heart."

3/They Expect Sacrifice

Scripture: *Colossians 4:1-18*

I

A wise and witty Englishman once defined an educated person as one who can do three things: (1) entertain himself; (2) entertain others; and (3) entertain a new idea.

We accept the first two without question: entertaining self and others. In fact, some of us specialize in one or both of them. But we will balk even as we smile over the third one: entertaining a new idea. That, even the slowest among us knows, is both difficult and dangerous. The very word "entertain" is misleading in this connection. "Grapple" would be better. The ability to grapple or wrestle or contend with a new idea until we have the true measure of its worth—this lies at the heart of an education. And it is the hardest and most exacting work we ever attempt. It is so much easier and apparently simpler to head for the stockades of traditionalism and conservatism each time a new idea comes up for bruising encounter. And some of us do just that—spend our lives evading, escaping, running away from new ideas, new experiences and new insights. Haven't you known people whose epitaph should be: "He spent his entire adult life in full retreat"?

Of course no one need live this way. The ones we honor in every walk of life argue the case too convincingly to need a verbal defense brief.

Prominent in this company are the heroic figures of Old and New Testament and those who have emerged at the critical points in the development of religious thought and life. They were not afraid to entertain a new idea; in fact, their glory lies in the simple truth that they staked their life on it—and won! But it was never easy, nor can we expect it to be easy now.

Charles Kettering, one of the leading research scientists of the automotive industry in our era, once said that the primary qualification of a research scientist is this: "He must not bruise easily!" I never read the New Testament or any other epic of Christian heroism without wanting to appropriate that qualification for a Christian: *"He must not bruise easily."* Certainly the men around Paul were able to take it!

Christianity has been described as a way of getting us into trouble and getting us out again. There can be no question about its getting us into trouble with ourselves, our group, and our way of life. That has always been true and, so far as we can see, it will continue to be true. It is no accident that the early Christians were known by their detractors as the ones "who upset the world"—though, it should be noted, the faith that caused them to try to upset the world had first upset their own lives.

When a student at the University of Chicago, a colleague of mine, majoring in ethics, was concentrating on the great ethical systems of the religions of the world. He came up from an intensive study of Christian ethics shaking his head and saying to me, "It demands too much of men. It is too hard, too uncompromising, too forbidding for ordinary people. It asks more than they can deliver and when they fail, it both condemns them as sinners and promises punishments too horrible to contemplate. We'll have to settle for a lot less than that."

Of course there is much truth in what he says: The Christian faith does demand a lot of us; it is uncompromising in its ethical ideals and standards; we may not be able to achieve them perfectly but we can and ought to be guided by them and be content to let the issue rest with God.

I cannot, in good faith, present the Christian way of life as an easy-going view of things that sanctifies our every whim, appetite, and desire and encourages us to live as we please. I cannot so present it because I have found the reverse to be painfully true. Nor am I alone in this. If I were, my own experience would not be worth the time it would take to relate it. But it is of a piece with Christian experience over the generations. Paul's experiences, as we have them in the Book of Acts and in his Letters, lead us directly to the heart of the matter.

II

Among Paul's many distinctions none is more arresting than this: *He spent more time in more prisons than any other man in the Bible.* He was a specialist in prisons; in dirty, cramped, vermin-infested holes; in stocks and fetters—heavy wrist and ankle bands with heavy chains attached either to the wall of the cell or to each other in such a fashion that the prisoner could only shuffle about or lift his hands with great difficulty.

Roman, Greek, or Jewish prison—you name it: Paul had been in it. He had been in prison so many times he refers to himself as a "prisoner of the Lord." I confess I am always appalled by his own calm recital of the punishment he had

40

endured. As you read the record slowly, let your mind and imagination reconstruct the agony of it all: "Five times I have received at the hands of the Jews the forty lashes less one." Five times Paul was tied up in the public square and given the vicious ceremonial lashings—five times! "Three times I have been beaten with rods; once I was stoned." Think of it! And as we do think of it, we find it difficult to understand how men could endure it.

I do not suppose that anyone ever gets used to that sort of treatment, but Paul learned how to put it to good use. Writing from prison (most of his letters were written in prison) he assures his friends, "I want you to know, brethren, that what has happened to me has really served to advance the gospel, so that it has become known throughout the whole praetorian guard and to all the rest that my imprisonment is for Christ; and most of the brethren have been made confident in the Lord because of my imprisonment, and are much more bold to speak the word of God without fear" (Phil. 1:13 RSV).

It is too much to think that a free-ranging spirit like Paul wanted or enjoyed imprisonment. But the truth is that he turned it to good advantage. It might brutalize some, but it exalted him! He saw great good coming out of those cruel experiences, and was content that it should be so. He was able to grapple with a *new idea,* namely, *God was preaching the gospel through his life as well as his lips.* Paul didn't need to be free in order to preach the gospel of freedom; he preached it with great effect wherever he was, whether in prison or outside.

Consequently, he closes his letter to the Colossians with the moving plea, "Remember my fetters." It is his way of reminding them not alone of his own suffering for the faith but of preparing them for a similar experience. Here is no cheap cultivation of sympathy. He is warning them against seeking an easy way to bear their witness. He is encouraging them to rejoice in the hardships that will come to them in their service of Jesus Christ. He is saying, in effect, "Follow my example; do not be ashamed to suffer for the truth."

There is no estimating how much sheer strength his letters poured into the fearful spirit of Christians during the three hundred years of fierce persecutions that were beginning to flame up all around them. When I consider that long stretch of almost unbearable human suffering, I wonder that Christianity is not more gloomy and forbidding than its light-hearted critics find it to be. When we say and sing, "The way of the cross leads home," we are not simply engaging in an evangelistic song, we are listening to the witness of the martyred saints of Christendom over two thousand years—beginning with men like Paul and, in our time, including men like Dietrich Bonhoeffer in Germany. If we listen humbly as Thomas à Kempis tells us of the "King's highway of the cross," we catch something of the glory of the cross, of suffering endured for Christ's sake and for the sake of the gospel. If we in our preaching and witness in the church sharpen the emphasis on sacrifice until it wounds our complacent consciences, there is good warrant for it in the experiences of Christians over two millennia.

The pattern of the stern demand for disciplined living has varied in many ways over this long expanse of time, but the demand itself has been and continues to be constant. *The Christian way of life requires discipline of the most rigorous sort if it is really to come alive in any of us: Discipline of mind; discipline of spirit; discipline of appetite, desire, and will.*

42

One of the most urgent questions before each person was phrased this way by a student in a forum last year, "If I really try to be a Christian, will I be very different from those who don't?" On the surface this looks like an ordinary student desire to belong to the group, yet retain identity; to be different yet not too different. One senior summed this up perfectly when he said, "In college we try so hard to be different we wind up being just like each other!"

The Christian life is not like any other life; it is identifiably different. The Christian family is not to be confused with any kind of family; it is identifiably different. Just so, the Christian church is, or ought to be, worlds removed from any other social grouping, however commendable these may be. And a Christian society—something we've dreamed about, prayed about, and worked for but never seen—will be a new way of life for all.

Once we get clearly before us why this is so, not only will it be easier to see why the adjective "Christian" changes every noun it modifies but we may be willing to subject ourselves to the discipline that makes the difference both possible and incvitable.

III

A Christian is one who openly and consciously accepts the fact that he finds the meaning and purpose of his life in the will of God as we see it in Jesus Christ. Loyalty to the Christian ethic ought to be nurtured by an ever-deepening understanding of it, and the firm foundation on which it stands. We ask no man to embrace any part of our faith as an item of blind faith. There is no place for conscious blindness in the Christian faith. We need to be able to give a reason for the faith that is within us if we are going to believe it and stand for it with our entire life as witness. Certainly we must not be like a certain politician who was challenged after one of his addresses with the question, "You say you don't believe in the Monroe Doctrine?" Immediately he answered, "Not at all. I would fight and die for it. All I said was I wasn't sure I understood it."

I am not trying to reduce our faith to a series of pat verbal definitions. What I am saying is that our understanding of it can serve as a sign pointing to a road that is hard to find and harder still to follow.

If we believe that we are the children of God and can live in a vital personal relationship with him, we will never again think meanly of ourselves. Humbly, yes, and always, but never meanly. Mob thinking, crowd conduct, and group morality will never be able to determine our thought and our life. Our ideals and norms for choice and judgment will lie far beyond those formulated by any group—they will lie, in fact, in our understanding of God's will as we see it in Jesus Christ and the claim it places upon us in terms of the problems we face today.

Of course this will not prevent us from living and working creatively in a group, but it does keep us from submerging ourselves, our ideals and values in the anonymity of a group. The age-old argument, "Well, everybody does it," should leave us cold as a legitimate kind of reasoning. If we do one thing rather than another, it must be because we think one is right and the other is wrong, or, at least, that one is more nearly right than the other.

Shall we not agree that most of the moral mistakes we make come about because we let someone else do our thinking for us, or have decided to "be a good fellow" and go along with the crowd? Young and old—we are all alike in this: We want group approval; we seek it earnestly; we are willing to go to almost any lengths to get it; we find it hard to dig in and say "no" in the face of group desire, if not demand. And this goes not alone in terms of the national groupings of which we are a part but of the smaller groups that loom so large in our day-to-day conduct and decisions.

We know full well how determined groups are to have implicit obedience of all their members. Group approval and group sanction go hand in hand—as Paul and his fellow Christians discovered a long time ago. It is a dangerous thing to break with a group for any reason. Our religious forefathers discovered that their loyalty to a new lord and a new life led them into new valleys of darkness, persecution, and terror. The prisons opened to them, and fetters were waiting for anyone who entertained a new idea that was serious enough to set him over against his group. Even as Paul warned his comrades to be ready for such unpleasant punishment, he urged upon them those loyalties that would surely draw down group disapproval on them and issue in that punishment.

All of which is a way of making a point that is almost too obvious to need elaboration: *Christian ethics is not the ethics for one who values group approval above everything else.* Rather it is for the person who is willing to try to find his way—and the judgment on his way—that comes through the will of God as we see it in Jesus Christ.

I do not mean that this as easy as a matter as opening and closing a book. But I am saying that it indicates an area of solid interest and concern that gives us something to think about and something to think with when we are trying to

45

think intelligently about the problems of right and wrong, good and evil, truth and falsehood.

Nor do I mean to give the impression that the Christian faith is a lone-wolf proposition, that it is every man for himself, that it causes us to separate ourselves from all groups with casual abandon. Not at all; but it does ask us to enter into or work for the creation of groups which hold all men to be the children of God and treats them accordingly.

Perhaps the difference can be pointed up in some such way as this. The family as a natural grouping of adults and children is not necessarily and inevitably Christian, even though love and sharing be part of the relationship. A Christian family will add to the tenderness, love, and sharing one thing more: a consciousness that these are expressions in our life of the love of God as we see it revealed in Jesus Christ. A Christian family is one which trains its members to be aware of and sensitive to the needs of others, one which plants in the hearts of everyone the desire to share and serve the love of God as far as he is able throughout his entire life.

Stewardship of life—that, I suppose, is the attitude that characterizes the Christian life and home. Our lives are gifts from God, trusts placed in our hands by him—and we must treat them accordingly. As precious as the gift of our own life is the greater gift of those relationships with others which give life meaning and purpose. A child will mature in a Christian home keenly aware that he is a child of God, that his life is a trust, and that he should use it as a channel through which God's love can be made more real in human life and affairs.

Obviously and inevitably there will be clashes with every

effort to foreshorten and limit this sense of fellowship and stewardship to some one part of the human family. And when the ethical commitments of his faith force him to move beyond community approval and commonly accepted limits and loyalties, the Christian will remember the fetters worn by Paul and every prophetic leader who has sought to follow the will of God as he has found it in Christ.

IV

Those of you who know something of early Christian history may think I am trying to revive the cult of martydom which flourished in certain sections of the church during the second and third centuries. Men actually invited persecutions and sought death in order to bear their witness. The cult became so attractive that church leaders had to warn against seeking martydom unless the great issues of the faith were surely involved in their sacrifice.

I am not interested in a revival of that kind of hysteria. But I am anxious to have us entertain the new idea that the Christian faith gives us a standard far beyond and outside any group and asks us to use it as a norm for measuring the degree of our cooperation with and conformity to that group. "We are called to be in the world, but not of the world," cried Paul—and that puts the matter perfectly.

Deep within us as the mainspring of our moral code and ethical choices is this personal devotion and commitment to God. It makes all the difference *in the world*. It takes precedence over what any group—however intimate or well intentioned—may say.

For all his cynicism and skepticism, George Bernard Shaw was hypnotized by this distinctive mark of the Christian. He explored it with sensitivity and understanding in several of his great plays, and the prose introductions to them, notably *Androcles and the Lion* and *St. Joan*. Shaw saw in early Christian martyrs and Joan of Arc a radical faith in God that literally transforms life on all levels. In these plays he broods over the fact that the main characters are impelled by a power other than themselves, are servants of someone who transcends groups, kings, emperors, and prelates alike.

This impresses me as a valid restatement of what Augustine, Luther and Wesley, and Paul were trying to say to their generations and something that each generation must try to say to itself if it is to hold high the standard of the Christian witness. Above all—let us not shrink from or shirk the fetters that are ours! Dr. Visser 't Hooft, long-time executive secretary of the World Council of Churches, once told a conference of missionaries, "The faith that is tested produces hope. It is one of the strangest aspects of the history of the church that the churches under pressure often know so much more about hope than the untroubled churches." That is why we need to say to ourselves and to one another: "Let us not shrink from our fetters!"

When we are tempted to do so, let us remember men like Paul who would hold high their fettered arms and proclaim that in their fetters they found freedom, courage, strength, hope, and the enduring presence of their Lord and Savior. More than this not many men will seek. And for a Christian, it is sufficient.

4/They Are Not Ashamed of the Gospel

Scripture: *Romans 1:1-17*

I

I wonder: Was Paul speaking for us as well as for himself when he made the magnificent proclamation: "For I am not ashamed of the gospel"?

Clearly he was speaking not only to Christians who were tempted to be ashamed of the gospel, but he was nerving himself up to one of the supreme encounters of his life as a missionary. In his assertion he does two things: he indicates a *problem* and he takes a *position*—and both problem and position are as new and as vital as the Christian faith itself.

The *problem,* to put it simply, is the temptation to question the relevance of the gospel to the momentous issues we face, to be ashamed of it in the sense that we think it inadequate to them, and, in consequence, to be afraid to preach it.

The *position* is to proclaim the gospel as the supremely important fact in life and history. Paul saw something we, too, must see. Christianity can be a force for the redemption of life only as we find our way through the problem to the position. To put it in pedestrian prose, we are called to fashion a Christian criticism of the total life of our day. And this in the face of the rapid spread of "No Criticism" signs posted over the grave issues of our time by individuals

49

and groups who either do not believe or are afraid to face honest Christian criticism.

I am sure we owe these "No Criticism" people a clear explanation of what Christian criticism is and why we make it. Yet we must remind ourselves that it is not a word to be spoken; it is a witness to be born, a life to be lived. And we must bear that witness and live that life—else we fail both God and man, and deny the Lord we say we seek to serve. This is no time for timidity in proclaiming the reality, the relevance, and above all the ultimacy of the will of God throughout the whole range of life and history. For this will be the standard by which we seek to measure the worth of what men do and propose to do.

II

Fortunately for us, our faith was not born in a social vacuum—nor can it be kept alive in one. From the beginning of its historic career it has been a responsible critic of the entire range of human life, for God's sake.

Never has this been done with greater power and adequacy than by the ethical prophets of early Israel. Amos, Isaiah, Jeremiah, Ezekiel: how grandly these names ring wherever vital religion is discussed! They had a single purpose: To stand where the ways part and keep their beloved land from choosing the path of sin and death and to persuade her to choose the path of righteousness and life. To this end they laid claim to the whole domain of life, for God's sake. They criticized morals, politics, foreign policy, and religious institutions. They held their country against the standard of God's will—and no power on earth could stop them. They knew the feel of danger, of stocks and dungeons, of public humiliation and private threat. But these happenings were trivial when laid alongside the tremendous fact indicated in the words: "The Lord took me," "The Lord spoke to me," "The hand of the Lord was upon me." Nothing human is foreign to our religious faith—this is the message of the prophets; and we may well hear in it a stern call to the permanent task of being a Christian, for God's sake.

The life of our Lord is too well known to require any elaboration on the point that he, too, bore his witness where the ways part for individual and social living. His life and teachings had and continue to have the effect of drawing lines in the minds and lives of men, inviting them to stand "on God's side."

When Jesus met the evils of life, he did not flinch, neither did he tone down his denunciation of them. What a bucketful of woes he dumped on the heads of the hypocritical religious leaders of his people! He could no more let the sins of his day go uncriticized than he could engage in them. And he saw what many of us are tempted to turn away from: *To let them go uncriticized is one way of engaging in them.* He was determined to put first things first, and he seems never to have been guilty of letting second things slip into first place unchallenged. When timid disciples warned him to be careful because of opposition, he replied in substance, "Fear not him who can kill the body, rather fear him who can kill your soul." He is a difficult man to know and to follow, but we who name his name and proclaim the gospel which we find in him have no other honest choice open to us than to try.

The great Christian figures through the ages—Paul, Augustine, Savonarola, Luther, Wesley—sensed the fact that they, too, were standing at the parting of the ways for their time. And they did so with such effectiveness that we measure them by the turn they gave history. Of course, they made many mistakes in judgment as they laid claim to the whole of life, for Christ's sake, but they never made the worst mistake of all, that is, of believing or letting anyone else believe that some part of life can be separated from the claim of God as we see it in Jesus Christ.

III

It is one thing to know and to remind ourselves and to explain to the "No Criticism" people the right and duty of responsible Christian criticism; it is quite another to accept the discipline of actually doing it. Paraphrasing the word of our Lord, "Straight is the gate and narrow is the way that leads to creative Christian criticism, and few there be who will even look for it, let alone find it." Yet understanding and mastering or being mastered by the discipline of Christian criticism can mean the difference between a witness of clear conviction and one of confused compromise in a day when there is too little conviction and too much compromise. The discipline itself consists in three general but well-defined steps.

The first step is a vital personal experience in which God lays claim to the life of a man. The prophet is God's man; therefore he must speak in God's name. The Christian finds God's claim in Christ, who becomes the light, the truth, and the way for him. This personal religious experience of God is the categorical imperative of faith, the alpha of all serious religious endeavors. When an early "No Criticism" man told Amos to cease his denunciations of the status quo, Amos told him he could no more keep still than he could ignore a lion prowling in the streets of their town.

This is the experience the mystic seeks to describe in his reports of the moments of ecstasy; it is the experience the rationalist seeks to report in his theology; it is the point in experience which the moralist has in mind in his endeavor to bring the ethical concerns of life to bear upon decisions that are to be made. It is, in short, the real directive of our faith in life.

It is far from being an easygoing master as every missionary can testify. When in South America a number of years ago, I was talking with a non-Christian who was attached to one of the universities in Uruguay. In the course of our conversation I asked him what things about the Christian faith made its greatest appeal to him. He answered quickly, "The sacrifices missionaries made for it."

The way of the creative critic is always thankless and, frequently, dangerous—but it is the only safe way for a man of courage and conviction to take.

The second step in the development of the discipline of Christian criticism is one in which our entire life is exposed to the judgment and mercy of the will of God. This is an endless, never-pleasant, and always humbling experience—a kind of living death, as Paul describes it. When we stand in the white light of his holy will as it manifests itself in and through Jesus Christ, no one on earth is more aware of our inadequacies, imperfections, and outright sinfulness than we are. We understand Isaiah's exclamation: "Woe is me! for I am undone." We literally feel the layers of conceit, pride, passion, and prejudice peel off, leaving us utterly devoid of the various protective coverings under which we habitually hide our own keen awareness of our creaturehood before Almighty God. We are overwhelmed by an acute sense of guilt, of sins of omission and commission hitting us

53

hard and all at once, like great waves racing for the shore and dropping squarely on us. This, I take it, is the experience our fathers called "the conviction of sin."

Fortunately, at the very depths of it, when we have and know we have no strength of our own on which we can call, we can and must call on Him whose last word for us is forgiveness and love. At that point and in that spiritual act, we recover ourselves, but in a new or renewed relationship as the humble son of him whom we hope to serve. We are never cleansed of our imperfections; they continue to cripple and haunt everything that we are and do. But we know them for what they are, and are given new strength with which to struggle against them. We are encouraged to believe that God can use us in spite of them. We are prepared to move forth in Christ's name and for his sake, preaching the gospel to all men. Always, over all that we say, there is the humble overtone of our awareness of spiritual purgation—and it is a continuing one—without which our witness becomes a sorting over of prudential admonitions in search of the least offensive compromise. With this experience, our witness becomes a humble proclamation that what God has done for one who is the chiefest of sinners, he can and will do for all persons.

Katherine Duffield, a YWCA secretary for student work, once said to a student gathering, "The most impossible and the most important thing in life is to know that the God of this universe can use even me."

The third step in the evolution of the discipline of Christian criticism brings the total life of mankind under the judgment of God. Nothing—no institution or idea or convention or group—is spared the ordeal of measuring itself against the ideal reality of the kingdom of God. And judgment begins in the house of the Lord! The Christian church must not ask to be excused from answering the question: "Does what you are doing square with the great goal of faith, the kingdom of God?" Church organizations, church practices, church customs—all these must be cleansed of dangerous sins which infect the very institution that seeks to purge the rest of society in the name of the kingdom of God. Fortunately for us, the tradition of unsparing criticism of ecclesiastical sins by churchmen is one of the best established facts in our religious tradition.

Nonchurchmen frequently and mistakenly infer that the church is one mass of homogeneous complacency, until and unless they criticize it. The actual truth is that the severest critics of the church in every age come from within her fellowship and, as a rule, stay within that fellowship. Theirs is a necessary task. Without it the church would soon perish of ethical and spiritual dry rot. But it must be done in every age, especially in an age of confusion like our own. As an indispensable prelude to her proclamation to other institutions and interests to cleanse their hands and hearts in the sight of God, the church must show the way by her own deeds and policies. She cannot and will not do this if her leadership is not continually measuring her against the goal of the kingdom to which she gives allegiance. Measure her disunity against the ideal of unity, and she stands convicted of sin. Measure her racial discrimination against the ideal of brotherhood, and she stands convicted of sin. Measure her compromise with the war system against the ideal of love, and she is one of the arch-sinners of the world. Judgments like these must be made—made in love to be sure—but made with courage and definiteness. Without them the church has no answer to the question: "Can the blind lead the blind?"

Although her witness is undeniably weakened by her sins, the Christian church must nonetheless bring the standard before which she bows to bear upon the life of the nations of the world today. For they, too, must be brought to the judgment bar of the God of the universe who holds the destiny of all of us in the hollow of his hand.

When it is clear that any given economic order, or some principle or policy within it, fosters conflict and injustice, we who stand at the parting of the ways must single it out for careful and searching criticism. We have no blueprint of an economic utopia, but we do have the guidance of the ideal of a social order in which mutual concern and purposeful cooperation lay the foundation for personal and social security. When we find trends afoot in our time which seem to be proceeding in other directions, we must bring them before the judgment bar of the ideal.

To the self-styled realist who demands to know what we have to offer that is "better" than the trend we criticize, we may say many things, but as Christians we need say no more than this to justify our right to speak—and to keep right on speaking: "This trend or principle or policy is going away from the ideal, not toward it, if we are to judge by its fruits of injustice and misery in human life. We, therefore, judge it to be wrong. We warn that to persist in it consciously or willfully is a sin against the will of God." To refuse to seek another and fairer solution of the problem it seeks to solve is not so much a confession of ignorance as it is a confession of guilt before God, whose holy will we refuse to search for "with all our hearts." Like Ezekiel, we may be perplexed by the further question which we will ask of ourselves: "But what good does it do to say that sort of thing? Proud, angry, and prosperous men seldom heed admonitions which spring from spiritual seedbeds." And it is imperative that we remember God's answer to Ezekiel that he was to get on with the job and leave the issue with God. For the conclusion always rests with God, not with those of us who have been called to preach in his name.

IV

Easily the greatest task we face today is that of trying to rebuild man's shattered confidence in himself and in his fellow men as reliable colleagues in the effort to achieve a world in which justice and law will undergird our common life. Of course, many difficult problems need to be worked out by diplomats and legislators, in the United Nations, in this country, and all over the world, *but the most difficult of all— in fact, the one underlying all, is that of building a basic mutual confidence in mankind including ourselves.*

Our so-called "mastery of nature" is turning out to be not so much a bad joke as a dangerous half-truth. A bitter Englishman was a lot closer to the truth when he said, "We have mastered the air only to be forced to burrow in the ground." And now we are seeking to master space and, as we do, in our present mood, we will find that our purpose is to jeopardize life all over the world. Eating away at the heart of all of our plans for world order and a new world of security and plenty is the cancerous suspicion that we are simply incapable of doing anything good, that the seed of death and destruction is implanted in any and everything we turn our hand and mind to.

It is the high calling of religion to reassure us at this point of deep spiritual doubt; to point out that the will of God is the permanent reality of the world, that whatever is in accordance with his will will live, that we have our clearest revelation of his will in the life and teachings of Jesus Christ, that it is our clear duty to seek an understanding of this revelation in terms of the problems we face today, and that we must commit ourselves without reservation to the endless task of seeking its fulfillment in human life and history. It is far, far easier to claim too little than too much for this answer. Without pretending that it settles specific questions about tariff, immigration, and taxation, it does provide an atmosphere in which they can be discussed hopefully and with justice to all. It does not answer them in detail; but without it, answers, however correct in detail, will prove to be purely academic.

V

Is not this the sum of the matter: we are called to preach the kingdom of God; to proclaim both its actual and potential reality in the life of man; to insist that all things human must finally square with it or perish; to awaken men to the realization that it is God's will, made in judgment and love, for all men; and that it alone will prevail?

We have no cause to be ashamed of this gospel. We do well to be ashamed of the many ways in which we dilute and compromise it; of the ways in which the church has forsaken it in so many of her practices; of the ways in which we ourselves sin against it. But this is not to be ashamed of the gospel; it is to be ashamed of the way in which we bear our witness to it, and is, in a sense, a left-handed tribute to our loyalty to the gospel.

Let us not be ashamed of the gospel of reconciliation when the only other gospel before men today is that of retaliation.

Let us not be ashamed of the gospel of brotherhood today when the only other gospel is that of suspicion, distrust, and strife. Let us not be ashamed of the gospel of love today when men are both ruining themselves and plotting the ultimate ruin of their children through the gospel of hatred and its implementation in the various weapons we are now making.

Let us stand then at the parting of the ways and preach the word without fear or favor; the word that "God was in Christ, reconciling the world unto himself, . . . and hath committed unto us the word of reconciliation." The Christian criticism of life is not a pattern of words; it is a way of life incarnate in the church as she struggles toward the creation of a world community which fulfills his dream for his disciples, "By this shall all men know that ye are my disciples, if ye have love one to another." This gospel is the good news of God to this and every other generation because it is the light, the truth, and the way out of our chaos into his peace. About this there can be no question, but each one of us will want to face in a deeply personal and probing way the questions of our fitness to live in such a community.

5/They Believe that Faith Works Through Love

Scripture: *Galatians 5:16*

I

One eloquent similarity between New Testament times and our own explains better than anything else why the New Testament is as fresh today as it was then, why it speaks as directly to men on Park Avenue in New York City today as it did to men on the streets of Athens in A.D. 57. Canon F. R. Barry describes it in these words: "Christianity was born into a world that was haunted by the suspicion that man was about played out." The truth of this is written large in the arts, philosophies, and religions of that period. Man had begun to lose faith in himself, in his ability to manage the problems that hammered away at him from all sides. He seemed to be sure of only one thing—the past. He was uncertain about the present; he was fearful of the future. A dark despair welled up in his heart, and he searched everywhere for either an escape from it or an answer to it.

Doesn't that describe us and our world to a T? It calls to mind a novel published a few years ago—*Going Away,* by Clancy Seigal. The central agent is a twenty-nine-year-old American novelist who is leaving the artificialities of Hollywood but isn't quite sure where he is going. Yet he is on his way in a red and white car racing along at top speed. "He is going away from nothing into nothing at eighty-five miles an hour." And he reports, "The bottom dropped out of my stomach with a straining hoarse fear." I think we understand what he means. Are we not searching everywhere for some way of grappling with and overcoming a similar despair, a similar sense of fatalism, a similar tendency to flee from where we are to some unknown place in search of a deep answer to our need? The Christian faith gives us the firm assurance that there is such an answer and presents it to us as it did to the New Testament world as the way to our salvation.

We shall surely be the losers if we flinch from the word *salvation* before we come to grips with its meaning. It has been in service a long time because it sums up one of the deepest and most persistent needs of the human spirit, especially in a day of confusion like our own. While the search for salvation is as old as man himself, it seems to have reached a peculiar intensity in New Testament times. Faith-hungry people were seeking it everywhere—in old places as well as in new ones.

There was no lack of answers to their quest—there never is! The early Christians encountered them on all points of the compass of their time.

They met the Jews who felt that salvation could be found through righteousness which they understood to be a life lived in conformity with ancestral religious law. Believing that in this law they had been given a sure knowledge of what God wanted them to do, they proclaimed obedience to it as a full answer to the despair that threatened to paralyze their energies.

The Greeks had another answer to the quest for salvation: wisdom. And they had reason to be confident in it. Back of them lay a five-hundred-year-old tradition of unequaled intellectual and aesthetic achievement. As they stood in porticoes designed by Phidias, they could discuss the plays of Aeschylus, Sophocles, and Euripides or the ideas of Socrates, Plato, and Aristotle. Why should they not glory in this tradition and believe that somewhere in it lay the full answer to their problems? Therefore, schools existed all over Greece for the specific purpose of carrying it on. As their troubles multiplied, so did their schools and the number of people who haunted the forums and street corners ready to listen to anyone who had a new idea or who preached "strange gods." They were sure that sooner or later they were going to hear *the idea* or discover *the system of ideas* that would turn the trick and satisfy their thirst for certainty and security both here and hereafter.

Then there were the Romans, overlords of that world, who sought salvation by still another route—power. How could they help believing in it? The legions of Caesar were the most important political fact of that day. Rome had a kind and an extent of power that gave many confidence that it alone could provide security. As their troubles multiplied, the Romans sought to meet them by multiplying the power of their legions, by extending the sway of their law, thus insuring the Pax Romana—which, for them was synonymous with salvation.

The early Christian met some new and strange answers coming from the mystery cults which had insinuated themselves in the life of all countries, *guaranteeing* salvation to all who were initiated into their mysteries. They promised everything despairing men might seek; cleansing from sin, victory over temptation, fellowship in a community of the saved, and triumph over death. Small wonder they had a tremendous following!

Surrounded as we are today by a hundred cults proclaiming easy salvation to all comers, I find real encouragement in the fact that our faith was not born in a spiritual vacuum. I rejoice that it matured in the fiercest kind of competition with other religious movements. It had to win or die, and it won the same way we must win today—if we are to win— by proving its superiority to rival claims in thought, devotion, and life.

And how we need to learn the way they went into the battle, openly, honestly, at the point of deepest need, and with the courage of great convictions! But let us never forget that it was a real battle they went into—a battle without quarter for the souls of men. If we will but listen, we can hear echoes of it on every page of the New Testament, especially in the letters of Paul.

II

Read his letters, and we are in for a bruising dialogue with one of the most intense men who ever lived. He was alive; he felt called of God to live deeply, passionately, devoutly— first as a Jew, then as a Christian.

His letters underscore certain facts we ought to face squarely. For one thing, *he identified himself with his listeners.* He stood where they stood. He had traveled every foot of the agonizing way through the grim wasteland of the spirit in which they were. He had the inner feel of their despair. He knew—how well he knew!—that they were looking for a way of faith, of thought, of life that most had not found. He sensed the anguish of the struggle that was going on in and for the minds and spirits of all of them. He was acquainted with the ways of salvation offered by Jew, Greek, Roman, and mystery cultist, and he knew they would not do.

Knowing the ones who paused to hear him preach, he was ready to give them the answer he believed with every fiber of his passionate being. And he was certain it was the only full answer to their quest. To put it in a word: the answer had come from God in Jesus Christ.

"He is the revelation of the love of God," cried Paul. "In him we see the full expression of God's intention for all men —and that intention is love. In him we can find a way of life that will give us a consciousness of communion with God and union with men that will satisfy our deepest needs. And that way of life is best described as 'faith working through love!' Men can be saved by this faith, can be born again in it, can become new creatures through it. It is freely offered to all and can be grasped by all. Let anyone approach Christ in faith and the Holy Spirit will surely take control of his life and guide him by 'faith working through love!' "

Over and over again Paul's consuming confidence in the power of love breaks forth in his letters. Recall the thirteenth chapter of I Corinthians! Reflect on his insistence to the Galatian churches that the Christian approach to life—or, if you prefer, the Christian formula for living—is to be found in these words: *"Faith working through love."*

Paul was not alone in his conviction that love is the key to an understanding of Christ, of God, and of our proper relationship with them. To a man, the writers of the New Testament stood together in their insistence that salvation could not be found by faith working through righteousness as the Jew believed, or through knowledge as the Greek believed, or through power as the Roman believed, or through mysteries as the cults believed, but only by "faith working through love." This was and remains to our time the open secret of the Christian gospel, the Christian life, and the Christian fellowship.

Paul and his comrades were alive to the misuses of the notion of love that were to cause Ibsen to write, "There is no word that has been soiled with lies like that word love." They were trying to tell the truth about the love of God as they had found it in their own experience. Love was no idle sentiment or casual idea for them. It was a banner raised in their heart and over their fellowship as they advanced to ultimate encounter with both the despair that threatened men and the false answers to it.

There is nothing modest or hesitant about their claim for this gospel. For them love is the key to the understanding of God's eternal nature and purpose; love alone explains the creation, maintenance, and redemption of the world. And it is God's free gift to all who will accept it in faith and live a life of "faith working through love."

III

Talk about a revolutionary idea! We have never had anything like the revolution implied in the New Testament emphasis on love.

The change in outlook it brought to the early world is not only immeasurable; it is almost incomprehensible. For generations men had been told that they were "atoms in a void" and, finally, many had come to believe it. When men believe that there is literally "no exit" for them, everyone waits around "for Godot"—or goes to Edna St. Vincent Millay's cocktail party "imbiding the pleasanter poisons" of despair.

Then came these indomitable Christian preachers proclaiming that the world was created by the active concern of God himself, that his purpose is grounded in love for all, that in Jesus Christ we have a full and perfect revelation of the meaning of that love, and that in the Christian fellowship this love is made both manifest and available to all.

Clearly the love of which the New Testament writers speak is not simply a human emotion; it is far, far deeper than that. As Clement of Alexandria put it, "Love is the motive of the whole divine activity," that it was "for love" the "Word of God issued forth to create the world," that it was "by love God sustained and guided it." This faith gave rise to the greatest definition of God ever formed by the mind of man: "God is love."

Some scholars see in the Gospel of John one man's triumphant effort to interpret the meaning of all this in day-to-day relationships. "Life is not immortality; it is a loving union with God and the brethren. Faith is love in action; knowledge, love in apprehension. Truth is not intellectual accuracy but moral honesty. Salvation is life: unity the fellowship of living beings . . . sin is disobedience to the dictates of love, a breach in the communion of those who live in one another."

Love so conceived is God's way of creating, maintaining, and redeeming the world. For it alone is sufficient to redeem man from despair, the sense of failure, that haunted him then and haunts us now.

Believe that God is love, that love is of God and, at one stroke, we banish the fear that we may be cosmic incidents, or accidents, or orphans. And in its place comes the luminous confidence that we are the children of the living God whose love surrounds us at all times and places, seeking to inform and guide us into the perfect relationship with one another and with him. Even when we, through the blindness of our minds and wills, become creatures of darkness because our deeds are evil, the light of the love of God still shines, showing us the way. And no power known to us can quench that light, though we can turn away from it. *Love never fails!*

The full answer of the New Testament preachers to the meaning of Jesus Christ is contained in one verse most of us learned in Sunday school years ago: "For God so loved the world, that he gave his only begotten Son, that whosoever believeth in him should not perish, but have everlasting life." This is the Christian approach to life. This gives us our clue to history, to the universe, to the things we are trying to do as a church, as members of the church, both in the church and in all our daily relationships.

Paul had it right: We are committed to a life of "faith working through love." And because this was revealed to us in Jesus Christ, we sing with Charles Wesley:

> Love divine, all loves excelling,
> Joy of heaven, to earth come down.

IV

But we must do more than sing about it. We must use it as an approach ought to be used—as a way of going somewhere. Only then can we hope to find a full answer to the despair, pessimism, and shallow epicureanism that rule so many of us. If we are to believe in the Christian approach to life enough to use it, there are certain things we *must* do. And the *must* is born of the experience of persons like us who have tried to use the Christian approach to life.

We must worship God in spirit and in truth, and worship

him steadily and conscientiously. We must seek him with all our mind and spirit and persist until we find him; then we must love him utterly and serve him devotedly. Then, and only then will we have the courage to seek our way in his will.

We must strive to know Jesus Christ at the deepest possible level of honest understanding—for he is our clearest revelation of the love of God. If we are to know him as the love of God come to light in human life, we shall need to know him as a person, to walk the roads in Palestine in company with his disciples. We shall need to hear him preach, to listen thoughtfully to his interpretation of life, relationships, and values. We shall want to watch him closely as he meets and deals with all sorts and conditions of people. We shall want to be acquainted with his high hopes and equally high fears about his disciples, for, in a strange way, we are among them. We shall want to pay strict attention to his teaching about the meaning of the kingdom of God and citizenship in that kingdom.

There is no point saying "we want to know him," unless we are prepared to go with him to the Judgment Court, to Gethsemane, to Calvary. And unless we are ready to do this, there is no use starting at all. As we accompany him through the final movements of his life we must gird ourselves for that prayer which comes closer to breaking the hearts of sensitive people than any one he ever uttered: "Father, forgive them for they know not what they do." We need to learn from him that "he that hath seen me hath seen the Father" and hang on to it for dear life until we understand it. In short, we need to know Jesus Christ as a person, and, as we do, we will know him as something more than a person, as the love of God come to light in human life.

Finally, we shall want to share the fellowship of love which binds man to man and man to God in and through him. To love him is to seek a relationship of understanding and fellowship with all men, beginning in our homes, our work groups, our churches. To love him is to reach out to all men in the spirit of compassion and concern, for he is the strong bond that holds men together. "I am the vine, ye are the branches," he said to his disciples. "By this shall all men know that ye are my disciples, if ye have love one to another." And then he laid it on the line: "This is my commandment, that you love one another as I have loved you." And the love of which he spoke was not a word to be uttered, it was a life to be lived and shared with men at the point of their deepest need and with God at the point of his holy will for human life.

It is a matter of record that "faith working through love" made all the difference in the world for Paul. Love gave him freedom: freedom from dependence on the law, freedom from despair over sin, freedom from fear of death. Freed from these through love, he became a new man whose faith wrote itself into the very structure of the Christian witness in history.

It is a matter of record that "faith working through love" made the same monumental difference for Kagawa, the Japanese Christian, who, long before World War II and before the upsurge of Communism in Asia, said, "Love is the basis of society. If we want to have a real society we need love. And when we want to put love in practice, then we come to the crucifixion of Christ. It may be very slow but surely it will conquer. You know how Christianity got the victory over the Roman Empire and the Roman Empire disappeared; but the truth of the crucifixion remains. The authority of kings and the authority of priests may die or disappear, but the truth of love stands forever and ever."

It is a matter of record that "faith working through love" made the same difference for William Temple, one of the greatest churchmen of our time. "The proclamation that God is love is not only a source of consolation; it is also a principle of judgment; for every purpose or policy that is alien to love and is based on selfishness or acquisitiveness is bound to end in disaster, because it is resisting the Supreme Power."

It is a matter of record that "faith working through love" continues to be the only honest interpretation of Christian living, both in personal life and in our life together as a church. It calls for understanding the life and the work of the church; more than that, it calls for sharing in it in the spirit of love in a fully responsible way. A church is weakened, not strengthened, by those who, however devout they may be, are sharp, hard, bitter and critical in their work. I have seen brilliant, competent people alienate themselves from the life of the church, not through lack of faith, but through lack of love. Lacking love, they lack understanding and a will to cooperate with others in the life and witness of the church. I have seen many others find a creative, stimulating home in the church because they were willing to let their faith work through love.

Somewhere in this area, we have the secret of greatness in a Christian church. A great church is made great by the greatness of soul of those who are in it. We may see the bigness of a church in its building or the number of its members, but we feel the greatness or the poverty of a church in the quality of its fellowship.

A large church is not necessarily a great church, although size is no barrier to greatness. A small church is not necessarily a little church; it may well be greater than its larger neighbor.

The real test of Christian churchmanship is whether we will let our faith find expression through works of love in our common life. To be concrete, each of us who believes that "faith working through love" is the Christian approach to life will find a place of service in the life and work of the church—in the church school, women's group's, men's clubs, young adult organizations, to name but a few of the doors open to us in the life of our fellowship in the church.

Let us enter into a covenant before the God in whom we believe and the Christ we are called to serve that our years together in the church shall begin, continue, and end in the great tradition of those who seek to let our faith work through love in all that we think, say and do. Let us be among those who begin and end each day saying:

> Take my life, and let it be
> Consecrated, Lord, to thee.

6/They State Their Faith Simply

Scripture: *Galatians 5:16-26, 6:7-10*

I

The passion for simplicity is one of the characteristics of our time. It is, I suppose, a reaction against the incredibly complicated technological material that is steadily being presented to us. Of late, we have had the various aspects of our rockets and satellites described to us in detail making us keenly aware of the fact that, scientifically speaking, life is becoming unbelievably complicated.

Many of us flinch from the word "geometry" because we have unhappy memories of our encounters in that field. Even so, we shall not find it difficult to come to terms with one of its key concepts, *axiom*. In geometry, an axiom indicates a proposition that is assumed to be true as we work at the solution of a problem. As we work at the problem, we have many different kinds of material, but the axioms guide their use in the actual development of the problem toward solution. Should we alter the axioms, we will have an entirely different problem on our hands.

Even as there are axioms for geometry, there are axioms for philosophy, ethics, and life in general. In these larger areas, axiom simply means a basic principle, a fundamental standard of value, the point at which we begin to think as we think about the many problems we must find answers to day by day. We always assume certain things before we really go to work on any realistic problem. And these are the axioms of life.

Of course, it is possible to challenge the axioms of life, to demand that they be reconsidered, and when this is done they must meet the challenge. Undoubtedly many of the axioms of our fathers are being severely challenged by currents in contemporary life and thought. That is all to the good; it makes our fundamental propositions stand up and give an account of themselves.

We might illustrate the matter this way. Formerly parents might say to children, "You must do as I say." That was an axiom for our fathers. Now we are likely to hear parents say to their children, "You must be yourself, do what comes naturally to you; you must be free." Not long ago an emancipated parent said this to an eight-year-old girl, and she replied, "Why do I have to be myself?" The parent is still looking for an answer, because the child had challenged one of the new axioms of life.

Yet the passion for simplicity is a valid one, and we will undoubtedly keep coming back to it as long as we live. At a meeting of the American Philosophical Association some years ago Dr. William Ernest Hocking, distinguished professor of Harvard University, startled everyone when he urged us to beware of needlessly complicated vocabularies and involved reasonings. He said, "If you can't state a thing simply, it probably isn't true!"

Imagine, if you will, the consternation that that kind of heresy would cause among philosophers and theologians! They, above all people, are the ones who never use a one-syllable word if there is a multisyllabic one handy.

Readers of history have relished Winston Churchill's great works. And I am sure we recall his dictum on the need for brevity and simplicity in official documents. When he became Prime Minister he ordered his aides to send in two kinds of reports: a very full report and then a one-page summary of the entire report in nontechnical terms. Churchill always began with that one page. He went on to the more complicated report later—but that one page was the point at which he started.

Somewhere in all this there is a hard lesson that we in the church must learn all over again. We need to state our faith simply and clearly in terms of the fireside and the dinner table if we are going to get a hearing for it. I realize that there are times when among the theologians and philosophers of religion we will be forgiven if we lapse into the technical jargons of our trade, but what is needed now is a simple, direct, axiomatic statement, both of assumptions and of what they mean in terms of ordinary human problems. That has been the work of the evangelist, the teacher, and the preacher of the Christian gospel from Paul's day to our own.

II

Paul's entire letter to the Galatians was written to a scattered group of Christians in one of the Provinces of Asia. Its purpose was to state in a simple, direct, axiomatic form the meaning of living as a Christian.

Times have changed, of course, since then so far as the church is concerned. The Christians who first heard Paul's letter lived in another kind of world than the one in which we live now.

The Christian church never had simpler social forms than at that time. There was no regularly ordained leadership; no real center of authority; no Bible as we know it now; no well-defined Christian liturgy; few, if any, Christian hymns and prayers; no complicated theology or system of sacraments. It is hard, isn't it, to visualize a day when men could not look back to a Wesley or a Luther, or a Calvin or an Aquinas, or an Augustine, or a Paul? It is hard, if not impossible, for us to recapture the "feel" of those early groups of the "followers of the way" as Christians thought of themselves, who were the spiritual ancestors of the tradition in which we stand. And they were spiritual pioneers in every sense of the word. They were discovering the simple truths upon which they wanted to build their lives and their communities.

The most pressing question they faced was, interestingly enough, the very one that is pressing us today: What is a Christian life? What does it mean to be a Christian? When I become a Christian, how is my life changed? What qualities of mind, spirit, and conduct should I strive for as I seek to live as a Christian?

Paul and his fellow workers never once doubted that their lives ought to be different by becoming Christian. No tempter whispered in their ears, "Go ahead; join the church—you can continue just as you are; no one will know the difference."

Paul insisted that to become a Christian meant to become utterly different from the way you had been. But his listeners wanted to know: how different?

It is this question to which Paul addressed himself in many of his letters and especially in the one to the Galatians, because he felt that they were being misled by Christian teachers who were needlessly complicating the whole matter and getting them terribly confused. It is a sobering thing to realize that Christian thinkers, even then, disagreed among themselves on how properly to live the Christian life!

Paul's opponents, in this particular case, were sincere Christians—there can be no doubt of that. They were Jews and they kept looking back to Judaism, even as the currents of history were rapidly carrying them farther and farther away from ancestral ways. Looking back to the axioms of their old tradition they said that the Christian life should have the same axioms. Consequently they drew up codes of conduct as had their fathers before them that consisted largely of what to eat, how to prepare the food, with whom to eat, and how to keep from being contaminated by the world.

Paul objected with extreme violence to this search for axioms in the background of another religious tradition. He insisted that the Christian religion could not be tied down to the precepts of ancient Jewish law. For him, faith in Jesus Christ brought release from all that; it made a man free to lift his heart with his hands to the power of God as something new and fresh. It enabled him to become a new creature in Christ and to share in a vital, responsible way in God's plan for redeeming the world. Of course, a faith like this would affect his life; that is, it would make him identifiably different both from what he had been before he became a Christian and from other non-Christians. Paul simply assumed that this would be the case.

Believing this, he draws up two lists of qualities of mind, spirit, and life; one of which the Christian faith opposes and the other that it embraces. "If you are serious about living the Christian life," he says, in effect, to the Galatians, "you must reject the one and embrace the other. You must reject the works of the flesh: immorality, impurity, licentiousness, idolatry, sorcery, enmity, strife, jealousy, anger, selfishness, dissension, party spirit, envy, drunkenness, carousing, and the like. You must embrace the fruits of the spirit which are love, joy, peace, patience, kindness, goodness, faithfulness, gentleness, self-control."

These constitute Paul's single page of interpretation, in the clear, nontechnical words of everyday life, of the meaning of the faith he spelled out in a much more complicated way in his letter to the Romans. The one thing we cannot say about these axioms is this: we do not understand them. We do. They are clear; they are fundamental; they are the axioms of the basic principles of Christian living in all ages.

III

Yet we must be clear on this point: the axioms of our faith are not sacred—even the most hallowed ones are open, and must be open, to criticism and discussion. There is, in other words, a time, a place, a way, and there may be a need to alter the axioms of our faith. It is the responsibility of philosophers and theologians to keep a careful eye on this and see that it is properly done. When our inherited axioms seem to complicate life, rather than clarify it, then we had better take another look at them.

Paul had done this with the axioms of his faith. He could not have become a Christian had he not challenged the axioms of Judaism. Whereas his fathers believed that salvation came through the law, Paul believed that it came through faith in Jesus Christ. Whereas his fathers believed that salvation came through the chosen people, Paul believed that it came to and through all who believed in Jesus Christ.

As Paul moved into the new world of the Christian faith, he discovered at least three great axioms that dominated his thought and his life. *First,* the love of God as he had found it and been found by it in Jesus Christ; *second,* God's claim on him in Jesus Christ; *third,* his conviction that the Christian life will be known by the qualities of love, joy, peace, patience, kindness, goodness, faithfulness, gentleness, and self-control.

We do not know how the Galatian Christians reacted when they read these lines. At least, here was something they could understand, strive for, and share with others. Here was the goal of their individual and corporate efforts to live the Christian life and preach the Christian gospel. Not that these axioms made being a Christian easy for them— that was not true—but they did make it clear to them. Paul's words opened up a road through the jungle of opinion, heresy, and uncertainty in which they had been groping for so long. Already convinced of God's call to them in Christ, they now knew what they were supposed to do about it. Paul had suggested to them the new axioms of Christian living.

Nor were the Galatians the last to profit by Paul's plain searching words. Time and again over succeeding centuries, confused Christians like ourselves have gone back to these spiritual axioms for a new sense of purpose in life. As much as anything else they keep the church human, alive, growing, in close touch with the daily lives of ordinary people. They do not speak of some far-off heaven which we may attain after death; they speak of life, here and now, among people like ourselves as it ought to be, under God.

I think it possible to sum up the importance of these axioms in some such way as this.

IV

First, *they describe Christian character.* Whatever else Christian living may be, it is not going through life with a set grin on our face like a Cheshire cat! It is not a generalized, shapeless goodwill that knows neither whence it comes, nor where it goes. The Christian life is a certain kind of life; *it rejects some attitudes and relationships as evil and embraces others as good.* The reason for rejecting some, and embracing others, is one and the same: faith in the will of God as revealed in Jesus Christ. Christian character, then, is always an expression, in life, of the Christian faith in the will of God; it is an attempt to interpret in life the purpose of God as we glimpse that purpose in Jesus Christ. Paul, let us recall, did not say to men generally, "Here, live this way." But to those who professed to be Christians he said, "Walk in the spirit. If your religion is sincere, you will try to live this kind of life." Paul well understood the words which Jesus spoke to his disciples, "Not everyone that saith unto me, Lord, Lord, shall enter into the kingdom. . . . By their fruits ye shall know them." The Christian character is one that is blessed by certain qualities: love, joy, peace, patience, kindness, goodness, faithfulness, gentleness, and self-control. Sow the axioms of the Christian life as seeds in our heart, we will reap them in terms of qualities like these. Paul tried to keep his fellow Christians alive to what their life should be, the qualities that men would encounter when they met them.

The axioms that we find in Paul describe the Christian fellowship. The purpose of God no more exhausts itself in individuals alone than life is limited to individuals alone. If God has a purpose for the individual, then he has one for the group and for society as well. That is why the Christian faith has talked and must continue to talk about the kingdom of God as a fundamental goal and objective of personal and corporate living. It comes down to this quite simple proposition: Christianity ought to make a difference in the person and in the group.

Which is a way of saying that communities of Christians, called churches, ought to be identifiably different in spirit, in tone and quality of life from any other institution or community in which we share. That is hard to believe, isn't it? It was hard then, and it is hard now. For if any one thing is plain in the fellowship of churches, it is the humanity of those of us who share in it.

It was true in Paul's day. Read any of his letters and we discover the humanness of the churches he founded. He was always deeply distressed by the squabbling he discovered among them. There was rivalry between, and among, influential people. There was trouble in families; between husbands and wives, parents and children. There was trouble about disorder in the services of worship. There were, upon occasion, shocking immoralities in the fellowship. How Paul hated it when he heard that some of his converts had actually taken one of their disputes to a pagan judge for settlement!

Paul did more than shake his head over these evils in the churches; he confronted those he once called his "unfinished" Christians with the ideal of a creative, redemptive Christian fellowship in which the love of God would be the standard by which they measured their relationship with one another. He urged them to set every evil in their lives over against the background of God's will for judgment. He urged them to seek the fulfillment of God's will for their lives. He believed with all his passionate soul that the Christian church had to bear its witness, as a church, to the love of God. He made it clear that churches as churches, as well as Christians as individuals, were to preach the word through love, joy, peace, patience, kindness, goodness, faithfulness, gentleness, and self-control. He said to churches, as he said to individuals, "Sow these as seeds in the life of your fellowship and you will reap their fruit in an effective witness for Jesus Christ. For whatever a church sows that it will also reap."

V

The main objections to Paul's axioms for Christian living are familiar to us. Obviously, and instantaneously, the proud old Greeks and Romans despised most of them as being weak. These so-called Christian virtues will make for weak men not strong men, the ancients thought. They continued their attack by saying, "Let a man take these Christian virtues seriously, and he will find himself better fitted to retreat from the world than to live creatively in the world, much less to overcome the world. If you are going to overcome the world you must have pride, courage, and just plain drive. These are essential to achievement, these are the real axioms for me." And so the classical thinkers urged upon individual Christians and Christian communities the need to be tough, spiritually tough, and strong in every way if they were going to overcome the world.

Later thinkers have said this in their own way, none more eloquently than Nietzsche, the dark genius of the nineteenth century. Power worshipers in our time are saying—or inferring it. We are power mad these days as we do our thinking about human relations. And not a few among us in churches appear to have more faith in the criticisms than in the axioms; in Nietzsche than in Paul.

Let us look for a moment at the charge that these axioms of Christian living will make for soft people.

Is it true that we go soft, ethically and morally speaking,

if we take seriously the axioms that God is love, that God has called us to a new life through faith in Christ, that this life is to be known by that remarkable array of qualities—love, joy, peace, patience, kindness, goodness, faithfulness, gentleness, and self-control? If so, we might expect that the most perfect embodiments of them in our tradition have been the softest people we have any record of. But is that the case?

Take Jesus Christ. It is true that he did not lead an armed revolt against the power of Rome. It is true that he did not organize the Jews into an armed band and descend upon Jerusalem and take possession of the city and sweep it clean. But does this mean that he was a weak character? We know of no firmer, more decisive, more creative life than his anywhere in the annals of human history. His love never failed and his steps never faltered, even though his pathway led to a confrontation with hatred, pain, and death. Love (his awareness of the love of God and his own love for men) did not weaken him; it gave him strength, courage, and direction as he needed them. It sustained him to the end. Most emphatically, Jesus Christ is not to be numbered among "the world's poor routed leavings" of whom Matthew Arnold wrote so eloquently.

St. Francis of Assisi is another example. Chuckle if you will over his peculiarities—and he had many—but no historian passes lightly over the way his influence brought both the Imperial Church and the Imperial Courts of Europe under scathing moral judgments. When Francis met rich men who gloried in their wealth he pointed out the poverty of their souls. When he came into the Papal Court he neither noticed nor was he impressed by the majesty of it. He might have asked for money, or arms, or other gifts at the disposal of the Pontiff, but all he asked was permission to serve the church by devoting himself to a life of poverty and usefulness wherever he could be of help. "Obviously mad," men whispered—until many years later they realized that he, more than any other man living at that time, had tided the church over one of her hardest periods. Soft, you say! Ask the crusaders who vied for his company on the long, rigorous journey to the Holy Land because serenity, peace, and joy seemed to accompany him like guardian angels. Ask the Sultan of the hosts of Islam whom they met there, into whose presence he came alone, unarmed, trying simply to persuade him, the head of the Mohammedans, to become a Christian! If that is what we mean by "softness," we might well pray God for a rebirth of it in the lives of most of us!

Others in our own time will come to mind as we think of the strength of character that comes through the embodiment of the Christian axioms for living. I think particularly of the late Muriel Lester, easily one of the great Christian leaders of our time. She was a small, quiet, shy, and very humble person, but I never heard anyone speak of her as being ethically and morally soft. She was the founder of a famous settlement house in London; half a dozen times she went around the world, always identifying herself as a champion of the poor and the underprivileged; she was a fearless outspoken advocate of peace all her mature life; she was so obviously a thorn in the side of the imperial policy of Britain that that government not only refused to let her come to the United States in 1940 because "she does the cause of our Empire no good," but they actually threw her in jail in Trinidad for a long period of time. Now, I ask you, does this sound like someone who lacks courage, direction, power? Muriel Lester went to Russia and China when it was both dangerous and highly suspect to go either place. She brought back an honest critical report of what she found there. She visited this country many times, both during and after World War II—always with a gracious gentleness that covered a steely kind of ethical and moral firmness in her makeup. When we think of Muriel Lester we realize that the Christian axioms, taken seriously, produce a kind of firmness in character, a kind of clarity in insight, a kind of definiteness in purpose for living that most of us lack and all of us want.

Now push the question one step further: Is it true that if the Christian church dedicates itself to the realization of these axioms it will become a spineless, pointless form of retreat from the great issues of our day?

No man who has read even so little as a page of history can say that. With all her deficiencies—and they have been and continue to be many—the church continues to be a power in human affairs. Her power, though, is peculiarly her own; that is, it is spiritual. The church was never weaker than when she had her armies and tried to coerce people into conformity. She was never stronger than when groups of people, confident in God, bore their witness to his purpose to the uttermost ends of the earth. Hospitals, orphanages, homes for the aged, schools and settlement houses, mission work at home and abroad—these are the fruits of the Christian fellowship that believed in the axioms of Christian living.

When we as a people confront the great moral problems of our day we should expect and want the church to be concerned, articulate, and influential in reaching the right solution. Churchmanship is not a matter, as some may think, of knowing how and when to keep discreetly quiet lest we get into trouble.

Great churchmanship is born with a realization that we

are called of God to find our way in his will as best we can and that our understanding of that way matures with our trying to find it.

Great churchmanship does not organize political parties, but it does address itself to the moral and spiritual problems of a people with such outspoken vigor and realism that existing political parties must listen to what it says.

Great churchmanship does not seek to govern a country, but it does bring its influence to bear in as decisive a way as possible in behalf of the moral and spiritual values that are always involved in matters before the government.

Great churchmanship is not primarily a matter of what I as a minister say; it is a matter of what we as a church do!

Deeper, then, than our elaborate ritual and theology, fundamental, even, to the broad foundation stones of our beautiful building; older than the heritage of our long and rich tradition, are these simple, searching axioms that ask us to be the kind of person in whom, and fellowship in which, love, joy, peace, patience, kindness, goodness, faithfulness, gentleness, and self-control reign supreme. With axioms like these as our guide we can find our way through any and every problem known to man. Let us not brush them aside as being too ordinary and commonplace to be important; for of such is the kingdom of God on as well as beyond earth.

7/They Believe that the Church Is the People of God

Scripture: *Ephesians 1:1-14*

I

The search for identity goes on on all levels of life today. We are engaged in it as persons, as a church, as citizens of this country, and as members of the human family. The answers we give to the nearer problems await the outcome of this search for answer to the ultimate one: Who are we; what is our purpose; how are we supposed to live in the light of that purpose?

Our search for identity sharpens one of the interesting differences between early Christians and ourselves. The New Testament is not so much a search for identity as it is a proclamation that the search is over, the answer has been found. The New Testament does not give us a closely reasoned theological answer on this. Rather it is a shout of joy, an invitation, hushed in wonder, to "Come and see what God has done for us and for all men in Jesus Christ!'

There is nothing modest or even humble about the way they exclaim over the discovery that he reveals the final purpose of God for mankind in general, and for themselves in particular. They do not so much argue the point as they proclaim it with a shout of joy. And, let me say, if we are able to read any page in the New Testament without hearing at least the echoes of this joy, we ought to close the book, lay it quietly to one side, and turn to something else—for we shall surely misread it.

II

We feel this in the opening sentences of Paul's letter to the Ephesians. He is reminding his readers of their joy in the new-found faith and then gives this glorious reason for it: God "destined us in love to be his sons through Jesus Christ" (1:5 RSV). How is that for a *destiny* and a *duty!* Better, a duty in which we find our destiny. Paul proceeds to amplify what he means in these stirring words, for God "has made known to us in all wisdom and insight the mystery of his will, according to his purpose which he set forth in Christ as a plan for the fullness of time, to unite all things in him, things in heaven and things on earth" (1:9-10 RSV). There we have it! The proclamation that in Jesus Christ we discover God's purpose for the world, the true meaning of life. That purpose is to unite all things in him. It is to see and to relate everything to God!

In studying the several possible meanings of the Greek words used here, scholars offer a stimulating set of interpretations. God is "summing up all things in Jesus Christ"; he is "bringing all things into a clear focus in him"; he is "uniting all things in him"; he is "gathering up all things in one in him." Perhaps it is my preoccupation with photography which draws me to one rather than another of these translations, but I do like this one: "The best sense in the passage seems to be that all things are brought to a focus in Christ. He is the focal point of the universe, of all history, of all being; all things, as they are brought into their true relation with him, are also brought into their true relation to one another and so into an all-embracing harmony."

I get the distinct impression that those early Christians meant business when they said they had found God in Christ and had been found by God in Christ. The one whom they called Lord was Lord in fact as well as in name, not alone of their life but of the entire universe. They were convinced that "the multiple strands of life, the entire manifold of nature and history, and all the particular blessings of God lead to one universal goal—a gigantic pattern of meaning, centered in Jesus Christ."

The very phrase "things in heaven and things in earth" is a picturesque way of describing the universality they had in mind. God's purpose for all creatures and all creation is seen in Jesus Christ—such is the faith of Paul and the ones to whom he was writing these letters. It is a little easier to see why they were unafraid of the wisdom of the Greeks or the power of the Romans; the God whom they found in Jesus Christ was the whole of which the philosophers and the Caesars were but parts.

"All this," they cried, "all this is of God! We have been called by God to this glorious task! The church is of God, not of man. The church is the people of God; the gathered family of God; the called of God. Therefore the church must place God and obedience to him at the very center of her worship and work."

Christians like Paul felt themselves to be part of "the body of Christ" on earth, to use a familiar figure of speech. The spirit of Christ found men separated from one another and from God and gathered them into his own nature. This, said Paul, explains our personal experience of being saved in Christ, and the being and purpose of the Christian church.

But it was clear to him that the church is not so much an organization as it is an organism, with Christ as head and heart; a church is not many branches and twigs heaped in a great pile; it is a mighty tree, deeply rooted in the universe, with branches lifted to highest heaven. The church is of God! In that is her destiny and her duty.

John Henry Jowett tells of calling on a cobbler whose home was in a little seaside town of England. The cobbler worked alone in a very tiny room. Jowett asked if he did not feel oppressed, even imprisoned, in the little room. "Oh, no," the cobbler replied. "If any feeling of that sort begins, I just open this door." And he opened a door that gave him a glorious view of the sea. When we in the church begin to feel our littleness, we need to open the door on God's glorious design for us in Christ. In that we see to the end of time and the ends of the earth.

III

This, then, is the answer—a hard answer—an answer we are either reluctant to study or, as we understand it, refuse to accept. It can be phrased rather sharply in some such way as this: When we become Christians, we step into a sacred community; we become brothers one of another; the closer we come to the One who is the center of our faith, the more deeply involved we become with one another. Jesus Christ finds us separated from one another and from God and offers us a new two-way relationship with one another and with God.

That is why it is the duty, the destiny, and the mission of the Christian communion here and everywhere to encourage us who are its members to reach out toward one another and toward the world in which we live and serve. We do this not because of our goodness but because of our calling, our destiny. Our being is our doing. We are not only known by what we do, we are what we do. We believe that the spirit of Christ which is the life of the church, has called us into this new relationship of love and cooperation. That is why we regard ourselves as a *"called community,"* not a *contrived community.* For this we are most grateful to the One who has called us into this unity and who has given us a work to do that is consonant with our calling.

This, then is our destiny and our duty as Christians: "God has designed us in love to be his sons through Jesus Christ." Paul grasped at once one of the initial implications of this conviction: *God "has made known to us . . . his purpose which he set forth in Christ . . . to unite all things in him . . ."* (Eph. 1:10 RSV).

This surely is one of the lessons we have been reluctant to learn, yet it is beginning to sink in on Christian churches all over the world today: Roman Catholic, Orthodox, Protestant, and even Baptist! It is actually probing to the heart of our ecclesiastical differences. It has brought to all of us a keen consciousness of sin.

And it is high time! Three hundred and fifty different Christian churches and cults, ranging all the way from St. Peter's in Rome and St. Paul's in London to store-front churches in Los Angeles—three hundred and fifty or more churches proclaiming Jesus Christ as Savior and presenting him as the unifying center of the human family—it just doesn't make sense! Who will believe us? Or should? The very multiplicity of our voices and forms reduces all we say about the unifying work of Christ to nonsense—unless we let it begin to unify our many, many churches. Never in the history of Christendom have our separated sections, Roman Catholic, Orthodox, and Protestant alike, been more conscious of or concerned about the shame of our separateness than today. We no longer think of it as an unfortunate fact; we regard it as a sin against God and Jesus Christ and confront ourselves with an ultimatum to discover how we can overcome it by the grace of God.

That is why, from its beginning nearly fifty years ago, the World Council of Churches has taken so strong a line on the fact of disunion. Those of us who have shared in some small way in the recent assemblies of the World Council are prepared to testify that the night of disunity among Christian churches is giving way to the dawn of union. Of course we have a long way to go, but the important fact is that we know it and are on that way and are determined to travel it to whatever end is opened up to us by God himself. We are not deceiving ourselves by thinking it will be an easy journey, but we are convinced that it is the journey we must take in loyalty to our duty and our destiny as the called people of God.

The ecumenical assemblies have had as their pillar of cloud by day and fire by night two great words from Paul regarding the nature of our unity and what it means in terms of present obligations.

IV

The first word is this: *The church is of God.* It is a *called* community, not a *contrived* community. The church, this and every other church, is not the accidental or chance creation of a group of people who happened to make up their minds that they were going to stand for certain things and

91

so came into a fellowship known as the church. Not at all!

The church was called into being by God in Christ speaking to and through men who found new meaning for their lives in that fact. They found more than meaning; they found a mission for living and the strength to carry that mission to the ends of the earth. The church was created by God in Christ to preach the gospel to all men. The church is sustained by God's love and power as it seeks to bear this witness. The church is answerable to God, primarily to God and finally only to God, for her stewardship of his will. Obviously, the church has failed repeatedly and fails today to do his will, but in his mercy it finds forgiveness and new commitment.

So churches the world over are finding a new yet old meaning in the very nature of the church, and they are saying, "We are the new community called into being by God in Christ, and we belong to the church not when our names are in the membership books of a local church, but when we feel deeply a part of the power of the love of God which sought expression in Jesus Christ and in the Christian tradition. Then, and only then, do we belong to the church."

When, if ever, we are tempted to dismiss all this as "words, words, nothing but words," we need to re-read the Salem Church Covenant drawn up in 1629 as a group of earnest settlers determined to leave the security of Boston and move deeper into Indian country to the west. Wanting to put down in writing a kind of Mayflower Compact of their own, they agreed on this: "We covenant with the Lord and one with an other and doe bynd our selves in the presence of God, to walke together in all his waies, according as he is pleased to reveale himself unto us in his blessed word of truth." The settlers who signed this document had a new purpose and God had a new voice in this new land. They felt just that way about it, too; they called themselves "the new Israel," meaning they were now the people of a new covenant. That is the way a churchman ought to feel about his church!

V

Now comes the second word which echoes through the Christian experience: *we are united in Christ*—yes, all three hundred and fifty of us are one. For the skeptic who asks for evidence we reply by calling attention to certain facts.

The first is this: Christ is the one through whom all Christians have found God. He is the one through whom all Christians have found deliverance from sin and death. He is the common Lord and Savior of all who bear the name "Christian." While "Christian" does not denote any one church, it does single out one distinctive fact: *in Jesus Christ men have found God*. Deeper, then, than any and all of the differences among our separate communions is this consciousness of sharing in the common Christian experience of finding God in Jesus Christ.

Even though this experience has found vastly different expressions in our churches, we no longer question the genuineness of the religious experience of one another. We accept it as valid and sincere. We regard one another as being good Christians even as we differ on forms of church polity and creedal structure. Though in our meetings we wear different ecclesiastical vestments, take communion in different ways, and hold differing theological ideas on many matters, we are always profoundly aware of our unity in Jesus Christ. This area of agreement is the broad foundation on which our various disagreements rest—and where, we are convinced, they will find their solution.

A second fact which we give for our conviction that we are united is our acceptance of the New Testament emphasis *on faith and works.* Though the books of that Testament were written by many different people in widely separated parts and times of the Greco-Roman world, a constant witness to Christ's unifying work runs through all. The Christians who wrote them felt what we feel today—that in him we are one. They said it many different ways—one of which is the passage in the Gospel of John which begins, "I am the vine, you are the branches." Another is Paul's famous metaphor of Christ as the head and the disciples as members of one body. In the thinking of Paul, Christ breaks down all partitions that separate men. Facing the deepest divisions in the life of his day with triumphant faith, Paul proclaims "there is neither Jew nor Greek, there is neither slave nor free, there is neither male nor female; for you are all one in Christ Jesus" (Gal. 3:28 RSV). If that does not settle the argument in churches over the sinfulness of segregation, nothing quoted from the Bible will!

A third fact which justifies our claim that we are united is the rapidly lengthening tradition of ecumenical experience and cooperation. After hundreds, yes, nearly thousands of years of occasional references to unity and occasional conversations about it, the churches have settled down to the discipline of exploring our interrelations. We have been doing this for fifty years and have discovered that the longer we have worked at this task, the more conscious we have become of the unity we actually have in Jesus Christ.

My own experience in ecumenical gatherings goes back nearly thirty years and, for what it may be worth, I can report a marked change in my attitude during that period of time. When I attended the first study group under the auspices of the World Council of Churches in Toronto in 1940, I recall being painfully conscious of the things that separated us from one another. But when I went to Uppsala in 1968, I was much more conscious of the things that unite us. Now it is a normal and easy thing to walk alongside colleagues from other churches and other countries as we try to find our way through common problems. This experience helps document the claim that "we are united in Christ"—that he has actually performed in our midst the ancient miracle of uniting all things in him.

Although churches have been reluctant to learn this lesson, we are now turning to it as the true meaning of the gospel for our day. Perhaps, by the grace of God and through his sharp proddings in history, we are realizing that in Christ he has spoken a saving word for men in the twentieth century as well as men in the first century. We are discovering that in the spirit of unity we do find the confidence that we need to address even the most momentous issues of the day in which we live. We are discovering that as we keep close to Christ we can hope to do the work of proclaiming the gospel in our life and time.

This then is our duty and our destiny, rather our duty in our destiny as a church, as a called community, called of God in and through Christ to be the one through whom his love comes to focus in the lives of men. This is a duty to be fulfilled: fulfilled in the face of the hard facts of personal and social problems—and we are the ones to do it to the very best of our ability. It will not be easy; it has never been easy; we shall have occasion many times to remember what we should never forget: that the central symbol of the Christian faith is a cross on which a man died in order to make all this real to us. *And there are still crosses enough to go around.*

It will not be easy for the churches to do their job, whether they are located in suburban areas or on Park Avenue in New York City. As we pursue our duty with realism and conviction, we are certain to discover the truth of the New Testament description of our forefathers, "They upset the world." One thing we know: we are not called upon to make ourselves or anyone else comfortable with the world as it is; we are not commissioned to pour holy water on the status quo. We are to preach the gospel without fear or favor, knowing full well that as we do it, it will "ruffle the fur" of a great many of us. But does anyone know how this sort of thing can be avoided? I certainly do not. I have come to the conclusion that fur has two purposes: it can be stroked or it can be ruffled. While we stroke it as much and as long as possible, there come times when it must be ruffled. Paul found this to be so in the first century, and I cannot deny the repeated validation of his point in our experiences in the twentieth century!

If the church be of God, then she must face the problems given her by the Lord of history in a fully responsible way.

In the World Council of Churches we have become better acquainted with the problems faced by churchmen in every section of the world. Some are very much alike no matter where men live, but others are quite different. Take the marked difference in some of the problems faced by us and our colleagues in the Russian Orthodox Church.

Russian churchmen face the threat of *hostility:* open, public, official, relentless, implacable hostility. We in this country face the threat of *respectability:* widespread acceptance as a symbol of well-being and acceptability to the power structures of our day. We are well thought of; we think well of one another; we think well of ourselves.

Russian churchmen are tempted to retreat from earnest confrontation with the grave issues, leaving that to social, cultural, and political forces; they are tempted to find or imagine they have found enough middle ground in the wide differences between Marxism and the Christian faith to live and let live.

We, too, are tempted to let well enough alone or to fall to our expected task of sprinkling holy water on the status quo, especially at those points where it is under most severe criticism.

"What a falling-off there was" from the first century when our fathers took pride in the charge that they "upset the world!" What heirs we have turned out to be! We cannot bring ourselves to upset the applecart, let alone the world.

But if the church be of God, as we claim, then we must bring the whole range of life and history under the judgment of his will as we see it in Jesus Christ. We do this, not because we think we are better or wiser than anyone else, but, simply, because it is our duty and our destiny to do it!

Even as the New Testament Christians looked the Caesars in the eye and said, "Thus didst thou!" we must look the lords of the earth in the eye and say the same thing—and keep on saying it as long as we live and profess the Christian faith.

We are supposed to gather all things in heaven and in earth together in Jesus Christ and for his sake. We are called to be the ones through whom the love of God is made real! We are called of God to take this gospel to the ends of the earth and to the very depths of the human heart and human society! And we have as our sole—and ample—reward the twin conviction that we are doing our duty and that we are not alone as we do it.

Membership in our communion is but the beginning of our involvement with one another and with the Christ we seek to serve and the gospel we seek to proclaim. I trust and pray we shall find ourselves in going forward together day after day, year after year becoming more and more unified in thought and spirit with one another, with him, and in his service.

This will not be easy—at least it has not been an easy task to date. Preaching the gospel takes of us the best that we have and all that we have. The final and most important lesson for us to learn is this: Trust God and get to work!

I am certain that it never occurred to Paul or to any of his churches that it was his job, not theirs, to spread the word in their city. Each one of them, upon entering the fellowship, became an ardent messenger of it to friends and neighbors. Each time one of us brings a friend or a neighbor to our church, or speaks a word of welcome to the church to new-comers in our neighborhood, we are standing in the New Testament tradition. We, the church, and our friend are all strengthened by it. This may seem a simple instance of how God is seeking to unite all things in him, but the church has grown to greatness through it. And can become great once more through it.

8/They Believe in the Future

Scripture: *Philippians 3:1-14*

I

For the past several years, the Committee for Economic Development, composed of two hundred leaders in business, government, and education, have held a symposium on some central question. The one before them recently was, "Can we afford tomorrow?" An issue of *the Saturday Review* carried several of the key papers presented at that time, and two of the ones who presented papers loom large for different reasons: one, the Hon. John V. Lindsay, the mayor of New York; the other, Mr. Irwin Miller, one of the business giants of our country and for three years president of the National Council of Churches.

As I worked my way through the papers presented at this symposium, I was struck with the seriousness with which these distinguished leaders asked and tried to answer the question, "Can we afford tomorrow?" Each one asked it from the point of view of his own center of concern in our time. My own first reaction to the question was almost flippant: "Why worry about tomorrow when we're not even sure we can afford today?" But a careful reading of these articles took the smile off my face. As I followed their thought through political, business, labor, and other issues, I discovered something that all but frightened me—I should have known it all along, but somehow or other these things slip out of focus once in awhile—namely, all vital issues are basically moral issues. I do not care whether it is in the field of business, or industry, or politics; all vital issues are basically moral issues.

This is what I mean: the ones who contributed to the symposium were saying many things but they all had an "if" clause attached to them: we can have a viable urban life *if* we want it and *if* we are willing to pay the price for it; we can have a social order of peace and cooperation *if* we want it and *if* we are willing to pay the price of it; we can have a world of rapidly decreasing tension and increasing concentration on common problems *if* we want it and *if* we are willing to pay the price of it. But the future comes high. It demands a kind of moral commitment that many of us simply are unwilling to make; not a single contributor to this symposium was sure that we have the moral fiber required to make the commitment that must be made. Each one felt that the development of this fiber lay outside his area, though the very future of his area was involved in it.

It was at this point that I felt again and anew the glorious trust of the church. For however we may care to describe the church, we are—or we ought to be—a community of articulate public concern on moral issues. If we are not willing to accept this as one of our primary responsibilities, then we admit that the church is irrelevant and quite undeserving of the time and the efforts of serious people. If we do accept it, we find ourselves stewards of the future, a future that is all around us. We've been *invaded* by the future; there is no way we can hold it off. The old days, good and bad, are gone beyond recall; the only days we have are today and tomorrow and the tomorrows that follow, and we are called upon to be good stewards of what is given us in time, as well as in our possessions. But as I get excited over this prospect, I find that we, too, must face the question asked by our colleagues in the symposium, "Can we afford tomorrow?"—the one that is all around us, the one we hear in the cry of every child, the plea of everyone in need; can we afford that future?

II

The writers of the New Testament, especially Paul, would have understood our situation. Their future had invaded their lives. They were asked to define a kind of stewardship to the future that would make their present meaningful. I like that word "steward" as it is used in the New Testament. The New Testament writers said, "We are stewards in God's house." And by "house" they meant their life, their possessions, their talents, as well as this earth. "All that we have belongs to him," they said. "We use it; he owns it. He entrusts it to us, he gives us real responsibility for the day, the talents, the opportunities we have, but we must never forget that we are always under him. We must make an accounting to him of our stewardship. Even as he has given us real responsibility and genuine trust, he holds us fully responsible for the use we make of what he has given us. He expects us to manage our time, and our day, with fidelity to his interests, not necessarily our own. His reward is approval enough for doing our duty; his disapproval is punishment for poor stewardship."

As I read the letters of Paul, I am sure he accepted this notion of stewardship, though he put it in a more active way than some of the other writers in the New Testament did. He

101

put it in terms of the metaphor of the race. Then, as now, when a race is being run, friends of the runner are at the finish line calling encouragement to him; he hears them, he bends every effort to win. "God," cries Paul, "is at the finish line of our life and we hear his call in Christ. In response to it, we ought to bend every effort to win; we ought to make every second, every ounce of energy, every relationship, count toward the end of doing what he wants us to do; we ought to forget everything in the fulfillment of our stewardship of the future as God wants it to be." He was writing to a very strong church in Philippi. He was warning them against something that weakens a church; he was lifting up the one thing that gives a church strength.

"The backward look is fatal to our faith," he said. Complete and utter concentration must be given to the work at hand and to the goal ahead. As he put it, "One thing I do, forgetting what lies behind and straining forward to what lies ahead, I press on toward the goal for the prize of the upward call of God in Christ Jesus." This is good advice for a runner who wants to win a race; it is good for us as we think of our work. The church at Philippi, I hope, heard what he had to say. And I hope churches today—nineteen hundred years after Paul gave his advice to the church in Philippi—will accept their stewardship of the present and the future.

The New Testament was written, and the Christian church created, by men whose lives were invaded by a new, unknown, and unpredictable future. Their lives had been upset by God; God had given them something to do, and they were reluctant to do it. As we thread our way through the pages of the New Testament, we realize all over again how hard it is to do the things that we must do if we are going to be stewards of the future.

III

Sometimes I wonder why Paul was so firm in his insistence that the backward look will prove fatal to Christian living. Isn't religion given to the backward look? Don't we surround ourselves with symbols that have meaning only as we look back? Look at the various figures in the mosaics of most churches. None of them are from the United States; none from England; none from France—all come from the Old and New Testaments. We look to them; we lift them up. Is that a backward look? In a sense it is, and if we want to get legalistic in this matter, I suppose we could have Paul in hot water, because he, too, had a way of looking back. Remember how he said, "If I want to look back, I can boast of being a Pharisee of the Pharisees!" And even in saying it, he was looking back. But Paul knew better than to think for a single moment that we could live the Christian life by looking over our shoulders. The Christian life forces us to look ahead.

And for this reason: when we start studying the past, we are tempted to wrangle over what should have been done. Once this gets under way, we fail to pay proper attention to what we are doing today. I've known people—and you have too—who can get so angry about something that happened long ago that they are unable to live today. I remember being on a faculty with two eminent scholars who disagreed so violently over their interpretation of Luther that they would not speak to each other. They reminded me of Henry Ward Beecher's celebrated dog who one day chased a rat into a certain hole, and could never again in all his life pass that hole without rushing and barking at it as though the rat had just dived in. If the backward look is the occasion for disagreement, dissension, and criticism of one another for things done and undone, it may serve many purposes, but there is one it will not serve: it will not help us get ready for the future. That is why, in the interfaith consultations going on now, we do not go back and start to figure out how we ever got separated. The point is not how did we get separated, but where do we come together now, and how can we spell it out in such realistic terms that we walk in unity with one another.

The usual weakness, though, of the backward look is not dissension, it is complacency. We spend so much time admiring the glories of yesterday that we are derelict in facing the duties of today. Here again, I suppose it's a matter of emphasis, but the temptation to stand awestruck before the remarkable procession of men in our past is almost uncontrollable. Each time I remember what was done by men like Paul and Luther and Wesley, I am tempted to say, "Well, we just can't do things like that anymore." Yet I am convinced that if these worthies could step out of the stained glass windows in which we entomb them in our time, they would hustle us into action soon enough. I often wonder what Wesley would think if he could see himself in a stained glass window—that's one of the things that never crossed his mind. There were too many people to be seen, too many people to be talked to, too many people to be preached to. He was the center of human relationships and a poor candidate for a stained glass window. I am sure of this: that while it is a good thing to let the glories of yesterday inspire us, it is another thing to let our vital energies expire in a kind of immoral admiration of what they did. We cannot grasp our future as Christians unless we are ready to concentrate on what lies ahead of us, and most of all, tuning our spirits to the will of God as best we can and fulfilling his will as faithfully as we can.

IV

The tasks we face, of course, as all realize, are tremendous. There are times when I wish we could just leave them to someone else—times when I wish we could just turn away from our responsibility as a church for moral issues, and say, "Let somebody else worry about them." But we cannot, and still be the church.

The good weathermen on television these days always show us at the beginning of their weather predictions a satellite photo of the weather all over our continent. Then they zero in on the limited place we live, and give us some notion of what we're going to be facing. This is a good strategy as we think of the future. We must do more than think of it in general terms. God has given us an age in which the old foundations have been broken and no man can put them together again as they once were, and in which we are going to be the ones through whom something new is created by the will of God, or nothing will be created.

No man is wise enough to say whether it can be done, but we know that this is our task today. And, as I study the work of the church, two words come up: *faith* and *mission*. The church must have faith and the church must be in mission. I cannot separate faith and mission; they belong together. Most of us know this in principle, but hesitate to put it into practice. As I think of our faith today, in a world like this, I realize that it is in my faith I find the courage to face the universal danger of our time—namely, annihilation, either in terms of some kind of nuclear holocaust, or in terms of the slow poisoning of the air, the entire atmosphere, the entire environment in such fashion that we can no longer live. We face annihilation. I know it; every human being knows it. Facing so tremendous, so pressing a problem—one that's creeping in through almost every channel, every breath we take, every place we go, every headline we read—the temptation to give up is very great. I confess: if it were not for my faith, which reminds me that *we don't give up,* I would be tempted to do so.

And why is it that we do not give up? It is simply because there is a source of strength and courage in this world which, if we link our lives to it, will make us adequate—yes, I am using the word I want—*adequate* for the problems we face today. We cannot do it alone; we must stand together if we are going to do it at all. And I am convinced that in the fellowship of the church we can do just that. I have never for a moment pretended that it was going to be an easy thing for us, but I have believed, and I still believe with all my heart, that in and through the church a saving word can be brought to mankind that will give us a new sense of courage, and hope, and direction. Unless that word comes through the religious forces of the world, I do not think it is going to come.

V

We are stewards of whatever future there is for mankind. That is one of the reasons why I believe so deeply not only in the church in general, but in each church as a part of the universal church. The work that is ours to do in our own church is a stewardship given to us by God. The opportunities given us are given to no one else, but we must fulfill them. The future that has surrounded us, that presses upon us, gives us many concrete ways of serving it and being good stewards of it. If we are good stewards of the future, we will be concerned about the future—not just as it affects us, but as it affects all men; we will do our thinking not only in terms of our todays and our tomorrows, but the todays and the tomorrows of all other men. It is the business of the church to give us a kind of worldwide photograph of the needs that must be met.

But we must begin here—we must keep our own church alive and strong, as alive and as strong as we can. I would like to suggest a formula that we might use: Let's not look around us at others and ask, "What are they doing?"; let us ask what God wants us to do, and be about it.

You will remember that delightful story in the last chapter of the Gospel of John where Peter wanted to know what was going to happen to another disciple: Jesus answered, "You let me take care of him; you follow me."

I suggest that this is a good place for us to begin our thought about the church. Let us ask what we are giving of time and talents and possessions in the work and the support of our church. Sacrificial giving is the way to shape the future—sacrificial giving of life, of time, and of talents. Each year there are two things every church must do: (1) It must ask its people to assume special responsibilities in the official life and work of the church. This gives the people an opportunity to practice their stewardship. It gives them an opportunity to say something that they alone can say. (2) It must ask for a pledge. When the church does this, it is not begging; it is giving the people an opportunity for a kind of stewardship that is peculiarly theirs. And if the church does this faithfully, it will go from strength to strength; but, should the church fail, it deservedly will get weaker and become less useful. God doesn't work in absentia, and neither can we. We cannot trust others to do what is ours to do— not if we want to be good stewards of our future.

Which symbol do we want for the church or the Christian in the world? We have a choice—pilgrim or grave-tender; people who are determined to be the ones through whom God's word is spoken or those who think that the work of the church is primarily to take good care of the past.

Is our future worth what it is going to cost? I believe it is! I believe it is better to have a little piece of a big future than a big piece of a dead past. And somehow I get the impression we're not alone! We stand together. We stand alongside unnumbered millions throughout the world through whom God is speaking and working. What more could we ask of life than that?

9/They Are Rebels with a Cause

Scripture: *Ephesians 6:13*

I

The letter to the Ephesians may have been written by Paul or by one of his disciples who regarded it as an introduction to a collection of Paul's letters that was being circulated in the early church. No matter who wrote it, it expresses in an unusual way the meaning of a practical, strenuous, useful Christian faith. Those among us who try to describe a difference between contemplation and action need to reread this letter. Paul knew of no such difference. For him the life of faith is a life of action and the life of action is a life of faith. They guard and validate each other. This fact is the heart of the letter to the Ephesians. And it is the kind of heart we need within us as we seek to be Christians today. Like all of Paul's letters the one to the Ephesians was intended to serve a very practical purpose. It exhorts its readers to prepare to bear their own witness to the Christian faith in the face of an increasingly hostile pagan world. It urges them to understand their faith, to advocate it in season and out, and to stand by it through thick and thin. It challenges them to get ready for the task, then to do it to the best of their ability, and, finally, to keep right on doing it no matter what happens.

The best known part of the letter gives us a picture of a

man getting ready for spiritual warfare of a most serious kind. Paul was telling his readers to get ready to do their best—and he meant "Get ready!" "You are," he cried, "to put on 'the whole armor of God.' Not just a piece of it such as you might be content to use in an easier encounter, but all of it." He patterns his advice after the armament of the Roman Legionnaire from helmet to shield to sword—and we must remember that the Legionnaire was the symbol of law and order in that day. Paul counsels Christians to "Stand therefore, having girded your lions with truth, and having put on the breastplate of righteousness, and having shod your feet with the equipment of the gospel of peace; above all taking the shield of faith. . . . And take the helmet of salvation, and the sword of the Spirit, which is the word of God." "You are," he continued, "to pray at all times, to keep alert, to contend against the whole host of spiritual wickedness which surrounds you." And he sums it up, "And having done all, to stand."

In this, he is not advising them simply to be stubborn: he is saying that only spiritual preparedness will steady their souls for conflict with temptation, trial, sin, and apparent defeat. "When you've done this," he says, "you've done your best, and that is what God expects of you."

Obviously, I would not be dwelling on Paul's advice if I did not think it as good and necessary for our time as it was for his. The formula for doing our best as Christians has not changed with the centuries or the continents. Here it is: *We must understand our faith; we must advocate it; we must be prepared to stand by it no matter how rough the going gets.*

These three steps cannot be separated from each other. *Understanding, advocacy,* and *determination* must go hand in hand if and when we do our best. Together they suggest an answer to two of the most revealing questions we ever face: "How do I know when I'm doing my best? Is it possible for me to measure the worth of what I do?"

II

These are not new questions nor are they confined to a few of us. Men have been facing or dodging them since Socrates urged the Athenians to "Know thyself." Many answers have emerged since then, and continue to get a hearing among us.

Some say, "Measure the worth of what we do by what others do and expect us to do." If we do as much as anyone else, we are doing enough, we think. Or we may say, "If I'm doing what everyone else is doing, I must be doing something right!" Slowly but surely we find that we are inclined to let others set the pattern for our style of clothing, our habit of churchgoing and church giving, our patriotism, and our morality.

Sociologists tell us that we are gregarious animals—which is a quaint way professors have of saying that we form groups that range all the way from intelligent, rational associations, on the one hand, to mobs on the other—with the mobs always being the larger, the more numerous, and the easier to join. Every parent knows how coercive a group can be on matters of dress, let us say, for a child from the age of six to a man of sixty. Children not only want to look alike, they begin to think, to talk, to feel alike. The mark of acceptability in a teen-age group, for example, is whether one conforms to the group. If he does, he's in: if he doesn't, he's out—he's a "square" or a "queer" or something else—meaning, he's not like the rest of us. To this day I do not know who is more to be pitied in the teen-age group, the one who pulls ahead of the others and is labeled a "brain" or the one who drops behind and is called a "slow." Both are looked down on by all whose individuality is safely hidden in the group itself. It's love's labors lost to urge them to be different. They don't want to be different; they want to be like everybody else in their group. They measure the worth of what they are by what others are; they measure the worth of what they do by what others do.

Nor is this the plight of teen-agers alone. Far too many of us keep right on using this yardstick after we move out of that period—some of us use it the rest of our life. If we do, we become the backbone of every effort to cast all men into one mold. We support the black shirts, the brown shirts, the silver shirts, the hard hats, and all other symbols of public conformity. We produce, support, and believe the propaganda mills that grind out the "acceptable ideas" day after day until men's minds are saturated with them. We are the victims of slogans repeated time after time. "Say it seven times if you want it remembered," we are told by one Madison Avenue firm. We are suspicious of anyone who differs from us; we are violently hostile to anyone who is openly critical of what we say and do—we cast him out as unfit to share the blessings of our society, our culture, and our country. "Love it or leave it," we threaten all who question what we do as a nation.

Sociologists warn us of the danger of this crush toward conformity. They tell us that democracy is doomed unless we can prevent the emergence of "mass man." By "mass man," they mean a society in which the individual is swallowed up by the group. Everyone who measures his worth by what others do and expect him to do is speeding the advent of the mass man.

We live in a day of "urban crisis" we are told on every hand. And, of course, it is true. We watch with great anxiety, we say, the burgeoning cities in which we live: we profess to be concerned about the crush toward conformity throughout our metropolitan life and area. Yet—we ask our schools to conform and to create people who are willing to conform to our society and our cultural structures. In a very real sense, the more we get together in these great urban constellations, the stronger the thrust toward some kind of ideational, social, and spiritual conformity.

III

There is another standard by which we can measure the worth of what we do. I find a very telling phrasing of it in the life of a Northwestern University student, Edward Spencer. He lived in the 1860s at the time when a lake steamer, carrying some 450 passengers, suffered shipwreck off shore within sight of the University. The ship sank quickly, carrying 350 people to their deaths. Spencer, a young student, led the efforts to rescue those thrown in stormy waters. He succeeded personally in bringing 17 to shore before he collapsed. The one question he was heard to ask, over and over again, was, "Did I do my best?" That, I suggest, is a yardstick by which we can really measure the worth of what we do: "Have we done our best?"

When we ask that question, we move into a different ethical and spiritual world from the one in which we measure the worth of our lives and work by what others do. This new world into which we move is the world of the explorer, the scout, the pioneer, the prophet, the saint, if you please. Such people follow the leading of what we, for lack of a better term, call "the inner light." They are aware of other people, but not awed into conformity by them. While concerned about the judgment of other people, they are more deeply concerned about the judgment of their own conscience and soul. They are individuals, so far as group pressures and judgments are concerned. But, interestingly enough, most of them are very humble and devout, believing in God, in his claim on their life, and seeking to serve him. *If they are rebels, they are rebels with a cause, the cause of God himself,* as they understand his will for the world. Which is to say, they are a peculiar breed of individualist.

Paul was encouraging the Christians in Ephesus to become that kind of person: men who find their sense of direction in the spiritual depths of their own lives, and then lift it as a banner and march under it wherever it leads. God's will for them is the "best" by which they measure themselves. The whole purpose of their life is to know and to do as best they can his will. From of old they have declared their independence of group pressures: We must obey God rather than men; you can kill my body, but you cannot harm my soul; I can do all things through him who strengthens me. Cries like these ring out of every page of the New Testament and, indeed, are the very stuff of great religion. They are echoed in every great life and moment of subsequent Christian history. They are essential to the church; they are essential to democracy; they are essential to a vital Christian life. Every institution, whether state or church, that tries to coerce men into conformity has been forced to hear and finally to heed these cries of rebellion.

IV

While we might speak of many men who exemplify this independence of man through dependence upon God, the name of William Wilberforce comes to my mind. He is just a name, if that, to most of us today, but it was not so in England a hundred years ago. Then Wilberforce was the voice of conscience to an England that had been content to tolerate and prosper by the slave trade; he was a strong voice of freedom lifted against the slave trade and in behalf of the Negro.

Wilberforce's life falls neatly into two parts: the first twenty-five years; the last forty-nine years. During the first period, he was a wealthy, gifted, young man whose sole concern was to get along as well as he could with his fellows —to be just like them. And in this he succeeded. He was highly regarded by all; he was elected to Parliament; he was in line for the many honors that lay ahead of a likable, successful young man.

Then came his conversion to what his biographer calls "evangelical Christianity" and, with it, the shift in his life from following the will of man to following the will of God. That shift made the difference that made the man.

Whereas he had at first tolerated the slave trade as "just one of those things" he now singled it out as a special object of relentless criticism and ceaseless attack. He never let up no matter how unpopular his crusade might be with the many who profited from the evil, some former friends and colleagues. He fought a long, hard legislative fight against it step by step—first against the slave trade, then against the institution of slavery in British colonies. Time and again the cause seemed lost, but Wilberforce never compromised and he never quit. Calling slavery a crime among men and a sin against God, he rallied an ever-increasing host of supporters until victory came—a victory that was no less complete because it was accomplished a few months after his death.

We will miss the greatest lesson of Wilberforce's life if we are content to say, "Here's a man who stuck by what he thought was right until he won." That is true, of course, but there is the deeper and more universal truth to be grasped: "Here is a man who, finding the purpose of his life in the will of God, found also the strength to pursue that purpose to the end of his life." In Paul's words, having put on the "whole armor of God," "having done all," he was able "to stand" and to keep right on standing to the end of his life.

V

It will take half a dozen Wilberforces to help us get on top of the drug problem today. Horace Sutton, writing of this problem in a recent issue of the *Saturday Review* used the title: "Drugs: Ten Years to Doomsday." And, as he sets forth the facts, the title seems appropriate.

Seven hundred seventy persons between the ages of fifteen and thirty-five died of heroin in New York City in 1970. Heroin kills more young people in New York City than autos, suicides, homicides, and cancer. In Philadelphia alone, in 1971, five times as many young people died of heroin as were killed in Vietnam. In New York City deaths from narcotics jumped from 200 in 1960 to 1,000 in 1969. According to a rough estimate there are 22,000 heroin users in the secondary schools of New York City alone. And the cost of the habit drives poor people into crimes of every kind: stealing, prostitution, even murder.

It is not enough to know and recite grim facts like these.

They are common knowledge among ever so many of us. What we must have is an arousal of public conscience by men and women like ourselves who will volunteer for the job of being a Wilberforce in this battle. Only then will the wheels be set in motion on an international scale to curb and cut off the flow of drugs into this country, and the rigorous control of them when they are smuggled in. The United Nations can and is trying to take the lead in the control of this drug traffic; our government is becoming increasingly concerned about it—but what is needed is the continual needling by many firm voices of conscience all over the country until the problem is faced wherever men look. The thing we still lack is a firm and universal demand that the drug threat be met on all levels of life.

When we have done our best about it, it will be stopped—and only then.

There are no easy answers in Christian thought; there are no easy triumphs in Christian living; there is no simple way for a church to be the church. Spiritual preparedness is just as essential as ever if we are to understand, advocate, and stand firmly for a Christian life and society today. After too long a period of trying to be comfortable Christians, we are beginning to suspect that there is a permanent truth in an ancient warning to would-be disciples: "If any man will come after me, let him deny himself, and take up his cross daily, and follow me."

Our Lord did not make discipleship easy; neither did Paul, nor St. Francis, nor Dominicus, nor Ignatius Loyola, nor Luther, nor Wesley. These heroic figures in our heritage knew the meaning of spiritual preparedness. They knew, too, that we must keep it up all our lives if we are to be effective Christians. They knew that just as an athlete trains and must

117

keep on training, the Christian must train and keep on training for a life of Christian service. Through long periods of prayer, seasons of self-denial, periods of great sacrifice, missions of danger, they kept their faith down to fighting weight. They were in a struggle with spiritual wickedness, and they knew it would be fatal to get out of condition.

Sometimes I feel we do not sense, as they did, the seriousness of the struggle that confronts the Christian in our time. The Reverend James Keller of the Christophers once assured listeners on the radio, "You can change the world." And then he proceeded to tell how. "The one thing that terrifies the godless the world over is the fear that someday all those who believe in Christ will wake up and start acting their beliefs. Once that happens, most of the great problems which plague mankind will disappear."

More than the "godless" would be terrified if this were to happen. Many confessing Christians would be equally terrified by the far-reaching changes that would certainly come if everyone who professes it began to act on his Christian faith. But my difficulty with Father Keller's formula is the implication that it is easy "to wake up and start acting" our belief in Christ. We can become aware of the need quite easily, but we cannot meet it without undergoing the hardest kind of spiritual discipline of understanding, of advocacy, and of standing firmly for our faith.

VI

Whenever I read Paul's word, "And having done all, to stand," my mind goes to our sister churches in Russia, in China, and in every other area of the world where Christians are having a hard fight against conformity by coercion.

Whenever I am tempted to criticize the Orthodox Church in the Soviet Union because of what she did not do under the Czars and does not now do under the Communist regime —things I think she should be doing—I am silenced by the question whether our church could do any more than she has done if we were in similar circumstances. Since 1917 the Russian churches have stood firmly against the bitterest kind of persecution ever launched against a church by a hostile government. They did not break, and they will not break. They continue to stand firm. A solid core of those churchmen have learned that men who put on "the whole armor of God" can stand firm in the day of trial.

And what of us here? Have we nothing to prepare for? Or have we done our Christian duty when we defend the status quo; find the absolute center politically, culturally, religiously; shout for law and order; damn the dissenters; and cheer the hard hats on in their crusade? These may be important things to do, but God help us if they are the most important things we can think of doing in the name of our Christian faith.

You've heard the flip but true saying that's been going the rounds, "If we do not stand for something, we will fall for anything." That comes close to describing the spiritual plight of many of us, doesn't it? And there is only one real answer to it—the one Paul recommended: spiritual preparedness of a high order.

Knowing what we stand for, knowing why we stand for it rather than for something else, then standing for it through thick and thin—that is the meaning of spiritual preparedness. Without it we will find ourselves falling for one thing after another, veering around like a weather vane that obeys the strongest gust of wind that happens to be blowing. That is

119

the business of a weather vane, but it is not the business of a compass, which takes its reading from the constant fields of energy of the universe. What are we in churches supposed to be, anyway: compasses or weather vanes? Compasses, let us hope, but the facts are not conclusive.

We live in a country which is in danger of compromising or losing through the systematic cultivation of fear and suspicion one of her greatest treasures: a freedom of thought, speech, criticism, and dissent unsurpassed in any other country of the world. What does it mean in terms of this problem that you and I profess to be Christians, that we belong to a Christian church which from the beginning has believed in the power of truth to win the victory in any debate or conflict?

We live in a world of rapid, unpredictable, and, in many ways, uncontrollable change. Some of us face the future with a fear akin to hysteria. What difference does it make that we claim to be Christians, claim to belong to a church that is dedicated to the task of trying to bring in the kingdom of God in which all things will become new? We ought to stand for something—and that something ought to be the will of God as we see it in Jesus Christ, and we ought to stand for it with our whole life.

VII

We must face—as did our fathers many times—the question: How much does my faith, my church, mean to me? Am I satisfied with the appearance of religion, the form of a church—or am I willing to push into the depths and find the real thing? Do I want a vital faith, one that guides me in life and death alike? Am I willing to say, with the French mystic Fénelon, "Cheered by the presence of God, I will do each moment, without anxiety, according to the strength which He shall give me, the task His providence assigns me"? Or are we looking for the path of least resistance and greatest momentary peace? Do we want a vital church: one that faces the gravity of our times with high heart and holy joy? How serious are we about finding a faith that sustains us and having a church that is a power for goodness, a true servant of God and man?

These are not rhetorical questions, as we will all recognize. They cut to the heart of the matter. I think of a busy layman who said, wistfully, that he wished he had a strong religious faith, and wanted to know how to go about getting one. A friend—another layman—replied, "Get into your Bible and study, and get into your church and worship and work." "I wish I could do that—but I haven't the time!" was the reply.

"Haven't the time"—that tells the story for many of us. We want to find God in our spare time. We want to nurture a childhood faith to full maturity in odd moments. What, honestly, are we willing to give God and the church? Our spare moments? The tag-end of our energies? What's left over? What we can get a tax deduction on and nothing more? What we in cooperation with the Internal Revenue Service can give—and nothing more?

We do not really expect much of that kind of stewardship of time and money, do we? The fruits of faith are reserved for us not when we are doing the least we can do, but when we are doing the most, not when we offer our poorest, but when we offer our best.

Having offered our best, we have every right to believe that we will be able to follow Paul's advice, "Stand firm."

10/They Are Responsible Citizens

Scripture: *Philippians 2:1-13*

I

Paul's well-known word to the Philippians to "work out your own salvation with fear and trembling" has always arrested the attention of thoughtful people. He is not urging his readers to be cowards in the face of life; he is warning them of the ever-present danger of failure. The Greek word he uses for fear means "a godly fear" growing out of a recognition of the weakness of men, the power of evil, and *man's need for God's help*. Paul was sure God could be depended on, but he was not sure Christians would turn to God for strength and guidance. When he counseled them to "work out your own salvation with fear and trembling," he was stating the continuing task of religion and one of the watchwords of democracy, as well we know! John Philpot Curran was to give this watchword a memorable phrasing in his famous warning to eighteenth-century England: "Eternal vigilance is the price of liberty." Paul was talking about the salvation of the soul, Curran about the salvation of the democratic state. Both perceived the fact that the great ends of life are never won or held without persistent and responsible thought and action all along the line.

The insights of both men rest upon the simple truth that there seems to be no place for panaceas—magic cure-alls—

in either religion or government. The roadway of religious history is dotted with the debris of tens of thousands of abortive efforts to work out some "quickie" solution to the persistent problems of human life. And the same is true in the field of government. When a panacea gets loose there, a tyranny—benevolent or malignant—is born. It will flourish vigorously and tragically for awhile, then die. At least most of them do. The overwhelming majority flourish—or appear to flourish with terrifying intensity for awhile—but only for awhile. Although the most arresting examples of these political panaceas have taken root in soil other than our own, we are surely living in a fool's paradise if we think our soil unfit for their nourishment.

As citizens of a democracy we are reminded of the simple and terrifying truth that many of us appear to be looking hungrily for a man on horseback or a kind of benevolent Santa Claus—someone, anyone who will promise to relieve us of the responsibility of life under the tension of eternal vigilance. There is something pathetically human about this persistent faith that there must be some short-cut, some quick way to the solution of human problems that will by-pass long-range, patient, continuing effort on our part.

I think of Lincoln Steffens' story of the little girl who when awakened from her sleep cried, "Oh, dear, I've lost my place in my dreams." Brute facts do that. They awaken us from our dreams of short-cuts and remind us that we must work out our own salvation in personal, social, and religious life with fear and trembling both in religion and government. This we must always keep in mind as we approach the problem of the moral requirements of public leadership in a democracy. There can be no long-range hope for a democracy unless we understand and accept the peculiar meaning of the kind of citizen and leader it requires. It ought to be axiomatic that religious institutions are deeply involved at this point—for it is our duty to seek to create and undergird the kind of morality that makes possible the abundant life.

Since the Christian faith is concerned with human beings there is a natural and unforced relationship between the Christian church and the whole range of human problems that we face today. Every vital problem before men is basically a moral and spiritual one. It concerns human values, human relationships, human beings—and the way we live together. The church approaches the problems of democracy with a concern born of her love for God and man, and a conviction that we are called upon to build as best we can the kingdom of God in our common life. While the church must seek to live in terms of the social and political patterns in which she finds herself, she cannot be content with any as she finds them. In faithfulness to her mission, she must accept as her own the deep and abiding problems of the people to whom she ministers. That is why the Christian church in our country has been and continues to be concerned with the problem of democratic leadership. Arthur Holt puts it very sharply: "The modern church is working at the task of being influential in a social order which it does not desire to manipulate, but for which it feels a moral responsibility."

It is in this spirit that we approach the problem of the moral requirements of public leadership in a democracy. While it would surely be out of place for us to try to suggest the political machinery by which democracy should function, we, as churchmen, are well within our role when we talk of the moral responsibility that rests upon citizen and leader alike if this form of government is to endure. That leads us directly to the question: "What kind of people do we need in our quest for a democratic society both in this land and throughout the world?" In raising this question, I want to underscore the fact that no leader, however great and good he might be, can relieve us of our responsibility as citizens in the achievement of a democracy. By the same token, no one leader can make or break a democracy as firmly rooted as we know ours to be. It would take a whole series of ruinous choices to undo the work of our forefathers, and no one with an ounce of faith in democracy thinks for a single moment that the majority of our people will be fooled all the time into letting precious rights slip away.

Yet the simple fact remains that leaders—the right kind of leaders—are of utmost importance in the functioning of a healthy democracy. They initiate policies; they symbolize the ideas and the ideals of the citizenry of the country; quite properly we count upon them as ones to whom we can turn as exemplars of democracy in action. It is, therefore, a matter of great importance when a democracy chooses its leaders in an election period and lives with them while they are in office. A healthy democracy—one determined to maintain itself—will measure every man who presents himself for leadership against certain moral requirements. I do not think I am exaggerating when I say that these requirements are not optional except as democracy itself is optional; they are determined by the very nature of democracy itself. They apply to all elections, all political parties, and to all who hold positions of public trust and leadership in a democracy. Of the many moral requirements that might be listed, four deserve special attention.

II

The leader we seek is one whose word is his bond. We must have faith in his integrity, but not in his alone. There must be no credibility gap. We must have faith in the integrity of those who support him as well as those with whom he proposes to share his public responsibilities. It is impossible to exaggerate the importance of public faith in the integrity-pattern of a man's total life. With it, democracy is possible; without it, the democratic dream vanishes into thin air.

"Why is this so?" we ask. And the answer can be stated very quickly.

Democracy, fundamentally, is a matter of faith in the collective wisdom of men over a long period of time. It could not be otherwise and live. It must make allowance for short-term mistakes, which mere mortals will surely make because of ignorance, avarice, or passion. It not only can but must admit mistakes if it would live. And we have had to do this repeatedly. Thus, as an earlier generation was unjust to the Indians, we must seek to make amends for this injustice as best we can. This is typical of the functioning of a democracy. Underlying it is a fundamental faith in the long-range justice and judgment of the average citizen of our country. Archibald MacLeish put it correctly, "Democracy is belief in people; not just some people, but in all people."

The basic institutions in a democracy lean heavily on this faith. Schools, courts, banks, as well as our forms of government by means of elected representatives on the local, state, and federal level simply assume this faith in the common citizen.

Representative government requires that we finally trust

our elected leaders and the ones whom they select to assist them with the right to make decisions in our name and behalf. Obviously they must appear before us and appeal for this most precious right. *That is the essential role of politics in our common life.* In early American history aspiring leaders made their appeal in town meetings where it was a fairly simple matter for neighbors and friends to check their words and promises against their family and their known character in community life and affairs. But all this is changed now—and of necessity. What would work in colonial New England is wholly unfit to this great nation with 200 million people sprawling across a continent 3,500 miles wide. Now party platforms are drawn up; campaigns are waged; candidates speak at mass meetings, in motorcades, and over radio and television. These are essential ways of encouraging us to have faith in some man and party because we believe what they say; we have faith in them, in their public word, and in the ones who are supporting them. Therefore we give them one of our most precious rights—that of speaking in our name.

Under these conditions, either a man's word is his bond or the credibility of the democratic process is placed in question; is, in fact, blown sky high. If he says one thing and does another, how far can we trust him in any sort of dealing? As citizens we have not only the right, but actually the moral responsibility to ask of every man who offers himself for public office whether his word is his bond, whether he can be trusted with the office, whether he makes promises intending to keep them or simply to snare votes with them, whether he is strong enough to hold his word when the pressures of friends and colleagues begin to push him in other directions. To alter the metaphor, can we trust him to keep his hand on the rudder of the ship of state and point her in the direction he pledged to take her—or will he let other hands take their turn at the rudder and send her in other directions?

To me, one of the most severe crises of credibility in the life of our country today is the profound skepticism of many of us toward the public utterances of political parties, candidates for high public offices, and occupants of such offices. It is no new thing for us to be critical of men who seek office —that is as old as democracy, and a thoroughly healthy attitude. But what concerns me now is the widespread decline of public confidence in the spoken word and the integrity of public officials. It is not that we take what they say with a grain of salt—that would be understandable. But we just don't believe what they say! We doubt what they mean—and we question whether they mean it. I am but indicating a dangerous fact when I say that the credibility of public leaders is now at an all-time low. This problem has haunted every president since Franklin Delano Roosevelt, to my certain knowledge. The polls make it clear that official statements and denials no longer carry conviction to large numbers of the citizens of this country. It's been a long, long time since anyone took seriously the news briefings of our military leaders in Saigon or in the Pentagon.

We face the same contradictions in statements on the matter of how seriously we are to move against the menace of pollution. That means cars, gasoline, and busses as well as other industries. Are we really going to crack down on them? The President assured some of them that they would not be made to suffer. Yet twelve hours later Mr. Ruckleshouse, chairman of the antipollution efforts, said that business will have to fall into line behind his efforts to clean up pollution—or else. Who is to be believed?

The moral implications of this attitude reach far beyond the excuse of political expediency and strike a fatal blow at the very nature of democracy itself. Democracy cannot and will not long survive the collapse of public confidence in the dignity of public office and in the integrity of its elected officials. Nothing is more important for the future of our country than an immediate effort to restore confidence in the integrity of the public leadership. Compared to this, the so-called issues in any given campaign pale into insignificance. We can survive, at great cost perhaps, mistakes made on specific issues, but we cannot expect democracy to survive the corroding conviction that the word of elected leaders, especially that of the president of the United States cannot be trusted, that his integrity may properly be questioned for whatever reason. It is the firm faith of religion that a man's integrity must be beyond question if he is to deserve the right to speak in our name. We have a right, therefore, to examine the morality of any man who presents himself for public office. No reasonable person will ask that he be faultless—paragons of virtue are hard to find—but we do expect him to symbolize a very high level of personal and public morality. And this includes the persons he appoints or supports for other public offices. We cannot afford to develop a high level of tolerance for immorality in high places. The moment we do this, we sign the death warrant of democracy.

III

The second requirement we seek in a leader is this: *He must unite us rather than divide us in our thinking and planning for the future.*

129

Take a cross-section of America, and we see a people harassed by great issues pressing for answer. We see embattled pressure groups composed of sincere persons on both sides of every issue. And the problems are not small—they are long-range and large in scope—problems like these: (1) the achievement and maintenance of world peace and order; (2) the achievement of basic civil rights for all citizens; (3) a more equitable distribution of the essentials of a high standard of living for all; (4) the solving of the ecological crisis.

Obviously no one has immediate solutions for such problems. No one man, no one party, and no one election is going to solve them finally. But 200 million Americans thinking and experimenting with various ways of solving them will sooner or later come up with the answers. Yet two things are essential to success: (1) an honest desire for a fair answer—one that will include the needs of all men; (2) a growing confidence in the integrity of those who may differ with us in the search. It is precisely at this point that one of the indispensable moral qualities of leadership comes to the fore. A leader we need will have the capacity to stimulate the growth of mutual confidence *across* lines of division in a democracy. This calls for more than political expedients and the art of compromise, though these have their place and are not to be scorned. It calls for the determination to bring the more cooperative leaders in the embattled groups together in order to lift their conflict to the higher plane of general public welfare. If this is not done, the fighters, the unconditional surrender type of men, always surge to the front in each group and set the stage for long, bitter strikes, riots, and other forms of poorly disguised civil war.

It cannot be stated too often or too strongly that anyone

who seeks to win and maintain a position of leadership by playing one group against another in our common life is engaged in nothing less than a betrayal of democracy. Call it good politics if we choose, but it is decadent morality and spurious religion, and I very much doubt that in the long run it is even good politics. Does anyone think for a moment that we can afford to move into the ominous future with a lessening of confidence in one another? That way madness lies! To the end of strengthening our common life we must seek and train men for positions of leadership who understand and practice the art of conciliation, who know how to nourish mutual confidence in areas of tension. We have a right to ask of a man who presents himself for a position of high public leadership that he will accept this as a major concern.

IV

A third requirement of leadership in a democracy is this: *The leader must accept and exalt the disciplines of democracy in his own thought and life.* Our particular form of government rests upon a system of checks and balances and the distribution of real power among the several branches of government—the executive, the legislative, and the judicial. Even a casual reader of *The Federalist Papers* knows how our founding fathers agonized over this point. They well understood the tendency of power to become more and more centralized, resulting finally in some form of tyranny. Hence their determination to distribute it among at least three major centers. Obviously this has always been a disputed area —with the President frequently set over against the Supreme Court or Congress or both! Now we are witnessing a period of acute tension between the Supreme Court and the Congress over several matters such as religion in public schools, reapportionment, and civil rights. Yet there can be no easy solution of this matter—nor should we expect one.

The triangular distribution of power must be maintained, and it is up to our leaders to see that it is maintained. I am no student of geometry, but it is clear that when we remove one point in our system of checks and balances, the entire triangle of power collapses into—God knows what—but it will not be our form of democracy. Yet the temptation to do just that is always with us; we must have men in positions of leadership who keep faith with the basic intention of our philosophy of proper order in a democracy.

Probably the most difficult discipline of a democracy is the giving and the taking of criticism. Yet the right and the responsibility of criticism is the life-blood of democracy. No man, no office, no institution can set itself up as being beyond the reach of criticism. Not all criticism is fair and responsible, but we have less to fear from hot-headed, rash, hasty, unfair criticism than from all well-intentioned efforts to curtail it. When we are tempted to stifle fundamental criticisms of our way of life, let us recall the old bromide of the trained bear who loved his master so dearly he would let nothing harm him. One day he was so enraged at the sight of a fly on his master's forehead that he summoned up all his strength and struck the fly a mighty blow. The story concludes: he killed the fly.

A democracy without the right of public dissent and criticism is a contradiction in terms. And a leadership which seeks to evade or stifle public criticism by invoking the *non sequitur,* "You must trust me" is poor leadership for a democracy. Isn't it about time we threw off the habit of equating serious criticism with either personal malice or concealed treason? A democracy that does not prize and guard most jealously the right of criticism and its free public expression will not long remain a democracy. It will not be overthrown by attacks from without; it will fall by betrayal from within. We need citizens and leaders alike who believe in the ideals and the institutions of our way of life so deeply that we gladly trust them to competition with all other ways of life. If they are as sound as we believe them to be, we have nothing to fear. If they are not, it is high time we discover them to be the imposters they would be. This, as I understand it, is the meaning of a vital faith in democracy.

V

A final moral requirement of our leader is this: *He must be fully alive to the truly crucial problems confronting us at any given time and be willing to help us face them openly, honestly, and together as one people*. This lays upon him his greatest moral test. And no leader in this land has had to face a graver set of issues than the ones before us now. Yet, as I think of it, I want to restate what I have just said. As a people we have two kinds or classes of problems before us now: one is all-important, so grave and difficult as to be in a class by itself; the other group includes many serious problems that must be faced, providing always we get the right answer to problem number one.

Problem number one today is the avoidance of thermonuclear war and the development of the spirit and the organizations that will insure peace. Let us never forget that we live under the mushroom clouds that are now rising from an increasing number of places in the world. Time is not on our side in this matter. Time is running out, and in the precious interval that remains we must not only make no mistakes but must be willing to find our way to new positions, if need be, in the determination to find a basis for continuing peace.

Dr. Grayson Kirk, former president of Columbia University, once summed up this overriding problem in a brilliant article in *Foreign Affairs*. Writing on "World Perspectives 1964," he described the new setting in which we must do all our thinking about security and peace. He calls for a fundamental re-examination of our foreign policy in the light of rapidly changing world conditions. And since he wrote that article, the world has stood on end several times over!

I do not propose to review all of Dr. Kirk's recommendations, but do commend to you the question with which the head of a European state opened a conversation with him: "What is your opinion of the general state of affairs in the world?" This, says Dr. Kirk, is a "reflection of a profound personal need to think globally about situations and trends that might have an effect upon the basic architecture of his foreign policy."

To date, we have had few public leaders in America, save Senator Fulbright and some others, who have been willing to take a fresh look at many of the axioms of our foreign policy. Yet the leader fit for democracy must be willing to do just that. Dr. Kirk warns both Soviet Russia and the United States, "Given an irrational person in a post of high authority in either state, a world catastrophe could ensue; for today the head of a nuclear-armed state, in his capacity as Commander-in-Chief of all the defense forces of his country, has literally in his own hands—unchecked by any legislative mandate—the power to plunge mankind into an unimaginable abyss." And this warning is followed with a recommendation: "Our new policy period must be characterized by an attitude of resolute firmness whenever necessary, but this must be tempered with greater flexibility, inventiveness, and realism about the world as it is . . . the issues at stake are great, and the American people deserve from their leaders not only courage and candor but also sobriety and restraint."

We trust our elected leaders to be our eyes, our hearts, our consciences, and our wills, as well as our voices as we move ahead in this ominous world. And we must seek and find, if we are able, those who can do this with an instinct for the great issues and a willingness to face them and to help us face them in mankind's search for security and peace. And, should it be necessary for us to rethink accepted positions such as diplomatic recognition of the People's Republic of China, then we expect our leaders to have the moral courage to confront us with that need, however unpalatable it may be. Should it seem essential to peace to extend the nuclear test ban, to turn over all nuclear weapons to the United Nations, to internationalize and demilitarize all space explorations and projects, then we expect our leaders to have the moral courage to lay this matter before us in utmost candor. The period of peace through what Winston Churchill once called a "balance of terror" is now at an end —the balance has been destroyed, and the terror is escalating into strident emotionalism if not hysteria. The man we put in the White House over the forseeable future will confront the gravest problem ever to face a president of the United States. And he must make no mistake in his dealing with it over the years immediately ahead. He will need more than our vote—he will need our moral and spiritual support all along the line. No matter who goes into that awesome office, we must close ranks behind him as he takes up the reins of his power and our future and the future of all mankind.

VI

Can we—do you think it remotely possible—for us to find the men we need for public office: men of integrity whose word is their bond, who will unite us across the lines of conflict in our country, who understand and accept the discipline of democracy, and who have a sound instinct for the crucial issue before us and the moral courage to face it? Can we find men of whom it can be said that they are able to face opposition without animosity, criticism without rancor, defeat without despair, and victory without conceit?

Let me give it as my testament of faith in our country that I believe we can find such men, and, having found them, will support them as we seek not only to maintain and enrich our way of life but also to continue our leadership in mankind's search for enduring peace. We must not be dismayed by our "fear and trembling" in the presence of the issues at hand for in and through them the God of all mankind is seeking to work out the salvation of the world. It ought to be a matter of great rejoicing to us that he has appointed us to be among his instruments in the achievement of this holy end.

11/They Have a True Sense of Value

Scripture: *Ephesians 4:11-16*

I

The New Testament has a way of opening up problems that are of both universal importance and special concern to Christians. When Paul advised the Christians in Ephesus to lead a life worthy of their calling as disciples of Jesus Christ, he put his finger on two permanently important problems. One is the general problem of worthiness; the other, the specific problem of worthiness as Christians. Both problems will richly repay attention not only at this time but throughout our life.

Sometime ago a reporter was given the assignment of doing a story on one of the richest men in the world. Once in the presence of his subject his first question was, "How much are you worth?" His host hesitated for a moment then replied quite honestly, "I just don't know."

In reading this I was impressed with question and answer alike. How anyone could conceivably have so much money that he did not know how much he had is and must remain a mystery to the overwhelming majority of us who are able to know and do know what we have right down to the last fleeting penny. But it must be that there are such!

In order to get the question aimed at bigger game, let me rephrase it. Instead of asking, "How much are we worth?"

I should like to ask, "How worthy are we, and how can we become more worthy than we are?" It is still a matter of seeking our worth but in a much broader sense. The first, "How much are we worth?" is a question of material resources. The latter, "How worthy are we?" is a question of character. Obviously, a man can be worth a lot of money yet be quite unworthy of it. He can be a Tommy Manville or a Nelson Rockefeller. There may be a question as to how much they are worth; both are reputed to have an awful lot of money. But ask of each, "How worthy is he of it?" and the answer must be fashioned out of his life and his work.

We can inherit worth if it is limited to money, but we cannot inherit worthiness. Someone else can make the money and give it to us for our use, but no one can give us the worthiness to use it wisely. Worthiness is an earned degree; there is nothing honorary about it.

That is why any important inquiry into our worth now and in the future must necessarily reach far beyond our bankroll or lack of it. It must plumb the depths of our character, our very soul—an admittedly and unavoidably painful procedure—for few of us are really worthy of the greatest gifts we enjoy—gifts like life, the shared life, and conscious fellowship with God.

II

Life is something we all have—in varying degrees. What a privilege and blessing it is! The ability to breathe, to see, to hear, to feel, to know, to appreciate the unending panorama of color, sound, and quiet; the joy of work and play; the strength of life, the challenge of work—no matter how we put it, life is a great gift and a priceless possession. We have it, but do we use it in such ways that we are worthy of it?

This life we have and prize is never a solitary entity, a naked soul; it is the nucleus of relationships with others and finds its deepest meaning with and from them. Take friends, loved ones, comrades out of our lives, and we would be little more than disincarnate spirits spinning through the spaces of meaninglessness. If I should try to point my finger at the deepest drive in life, I'd try this: "It is the quest for meaning through the deepening of creative relationships."

Yet the gift of the shared life is ours both as present fact and unfolding possibilities. We have parents and family. We have comrades in work and play. We have or seek loved ones for a home and family of our own. But are we worthy of such relationships? Who are we, and what have we done to deserve the precious privilege of entering into any or all of them?

What student can help wondering whether he is worthy of the opportunity to receive a thorough college and university training? How I wish we did not take that for granted, as our due, as something someone owes us! Perhaps we would not be as casual about it as we sometimes seem to be if it should come a little harder.

Last year I asked a high school senior what he was going to do next year. He said, "Oh, I suppose I'll try college. My old man has his heart set on it!" Startled, I offered to intercede with his father for him and persuade the father to stop trying to send him to college, but the boy said, "I might as well go. There's nothing else I'd rather do." That, I submit, is a slight interest in a college education!

I found it to be quite different in Japan when I was there several years ago. Visiting half a dozen campuses, I found the most intense students imaginable. They knew they were fortunate to be in college. By a discipline of study that imperiled the health of many, they tried to prove worthy of that privilege and the unfolding privilege of responsible leadership in the life of their beautiful and beloved land.

I should like to suggest that no student or faculty member is worthy of his status on any campus here or anywhere else in the world unless in all humility he has asked himself, "Am I worthy of this opportunity?"

Every four years we in the United States must determine whether we are worthy of the disciplines of democracy so far as the exercise of our right of franchise is concerned. We cannot help wondering about it when half of our adults do not even take the trouble to vote. A study of recent political campaigns deepens our concern over this matter.

Unless I am wholly mistaken, the image of the American people as we see it in the dominant motives that are appealed to in political campaigns is cause for deep concern. What moves us: *fear, hate, pride, anxiety, security?* Or to spell it out a little more carefully, if we may draw proper inference from the appeals that are made for our vote, the things that concern us most are: (1) self-interest—my job, my income, my security, my future; (2) group interest—labor, management, religion, section of the country, minority status of whatever kind; (3) such world concerns as have included themselves in a serious way are dealt with under the dubious heading of appeal to prestige, power, and the will and the power to save the world, or to lead the free world, or finally, to overcome the enemy. We can almost count on the fingers of one hand the number of sincere gestures made to a real comradeship and a sharing of responsibility with our sister nations in the United Nations or with our neighbors in this hemisphere or our friends in other sections of the world in the spirit of conciliation. What I am saying is this: the image of America that comes through the appeals of a political campaign makes us wonder how worthy we are of the disciplines of democracy in this great country.

I find myself questioning whether we have lost our confidence in democracy when we begin to curtail the freedom of thought, speech, association, and utterance that hitherto have been among the brightest stars in our firmament. Yet we continue to take freedom and democracy as our due. We assume that we not only deserve them but that we can serve them best by looking out for ourselves, humoring our own interests and prejudices with only casual glances at the needs and perplexities of other people. Could Plato have been right in his insistence that democracy cannot maintain itself because of the selfishness of the individuals who compose it? Is it possible that we who talk so much about it are utterly unworthy of it?

III

Let us recall how Paul urged the Ephesian Christians to be worthy of their calling as Christians. He asked them to "grow up into Christ." He set before them and all who stood in the Christian tradition a threefold goal for one who would be worthy of his calling.

First, we are to strive until we attain to the unity of the faith and the knowledge of the Son of God. Which is a way of saying that we are to keep struggling at the interpretation of the meaning of our faith until we are brought into communion with one another by our knowledge of Jesus Christ and of what he means for us and for our life and time.

Then we are to strive until we attain mature manhood. By this Paul meant firmness of judgment, stability of character, the ability to bear "the slings and arrows of outrageous fortune" and not be deflected from basic loyalties.

Finally, he asks that we strive until we attain the measure of the stature of the fullness of Christ. It was a basic conviction of Paul's that as a man opened his life to the meaning of Christ, it would enter in and remold his life until he actually took on the likeness of Jesus Christ. This, said Paul, is what it means to "grow up into Christ," to live a life worthy of our calling.

Several things become clear at once about our Christian faith so understood. It cannot be inherited; it cannot be given or conferred upon us by anyone else no matter how close to us they may be. We must earn it by honest and unrelenting thought, by sincere faith, and by the total commitment of life to the Christian way. A life worthy of our calling is a life "lost in Christ," to use another New Testament phrase.

Before we turn away from this notion as of dated importance, something like an invitation to serve in the legions of the Imperial Caesars, we should consider what Dr. Gregory Vlastos, professor of philosophy at Princeton, once wrote: "To give one's life away to what one knows to be of the highest worth, not only for oneself, but for all mankind, is the most mature experience open to man."

The whole purpose of the Christian faith is to persuade us to give our life away, not in sentimental gesture, but in personal and social involvement in the pursuit of the ethical purposes we find in Jesus Christ. Only as we are willing to do this can we hope to be worthy of the calling of God we hear in Jesus Christ.

142

IV

Even those of us who are willing to grant the priority of worth in life need some assurance that it is possible to increase whatever worthiness we may now have, not only for creative personal relationships, but for facing great social issues. We need to have some confidence in our ability to make a great commitment if we are going to serve the cause of Christ in a day like this.

With an eye on the record, we can say with emphasis that it is not only possible, but that each one of us can and ought to do it. It is a high road, hard to travel, but it can be traveled, and it deserves the effort it takes.

The cultivation of worth seems to be more an art than a science. I know of no one who is able to draw up a set of specifications or steps that will lead us inevitably to the end of greater worthiness. But this is far from saying that it cannot be cultivated. It can—as every artist, scientist, thinker, and responsible person knows.

Zona Gale, the novelist, was once asked for her social creed. She replied, simply and profoundly, "I have determined to increase the area of my awareness." Look at that for a moment, and you may feel with me that this is much more than a social creed; it is the watchword of a creative life. It reminds me of what Henry James once said when asked how to pursue the art of fiction. He answered, "Try to be one of those people on whom nothing is lost."

This is hard advice—harder than we will ever know until we try to take it. Instead of being content to see what we want to see and to hear what we want to hear, we shall try to see all there is to see and to hear all there is to hear— which is a real undertaking. Only one who is aware of and prepared to pay the price of increasing and deepening sensitivity to human life and needs will even attempt it. And the price of ever-increasing sensitivity and awareness is high and hard. It is so much simpler, so much less painful, so much more peaceful to operate within the well-defined categories of what I like, what I want, what I fear, what I hate, what I believe. Simpler, I say, and for the same reason it is simpler to sail a boat in a well-protected small body of water than out on the high seas.

If we are proud of our prejudices and make a virtue of our blindness, then we will not care to explore the meaning of greater sensitivity and awareness and thus close out permanently the meaning of greater worth. We will be something like the big game hunter who had gone to India on tiger hunts for many years. He had learned much about the habits and customs of the people but had paid no attention at all to the work of the Christian missionaries—and, admittedly, had no time or use for the Christian faith. One day he met a missionary. Almost in self-defense, he said, "In forty years I have never seen a Christian convert." The missionary replied, "That's interesting. In fifty years I have never seen a tiger. You see, I have never looked for tigers." I suppose, in a sense, both men needed a greater area of awareness because there are tigers as well as Christian converts in India.

One of the very first—and possibly the hardest—battles to be fought if we are to increase our area of our awareness is strictly an internal one; namely, with our inherited and inherent prejudices. Prejudices as to race, religion, or culture build walls around us or, if you prefer, put blinders on us. They permit us to see only what they want us to see. They block out all else, leaving us conscious of the wrong things, i.e., of all that will support and of nothing that will contradict them.

In time of crisis, whether in war, depression, or great uncertainty, fear and hate apply for the job of doorman of our spirits. If we hire them, they will admit only those stories or ideas that will nurture our fear and hate. We have seen this in every war mankind has fought. In World War II we called and permitted others to call the Japanese and Germans by every disgraceful, hateful name we could find. We knew we were wrong as we did it. We knew we were defaming a great people—but that is precisely what we were out to do. So, in company with one another, we sinned against them and against the God who made us all. Just how deeply we sinned against them I did not know until I was in Japan, in their homes, schools, churches, and fellowship.

Will anyone deny that wars grow out of situations in which people are progressively blinded to the total life of one another? War is a massive social operation which can be carried out only when the moral conscience of mankind is totally anesthetized by repeated doses of fear, hate, misrepresentation, and continual self-righteousness.

The problem of awareness as the first step toward worthiness comes closer home when we ask how large our area of awareness is of other races, religions, and nations. Are we willing to become one of those on whom nothing is lost as we approach a Jew, or a Negro, or a Catholic, or a Muslim, or a Buddhist, or an alien, or anyone other than ourselves? Are we alive to them as persons, as human beings, as children of God—or do we have ready-made categories dug deep in our prejudices into which we dump and damn them all? Are we alert to the wrong things about them or are we willing to try to cultivate an alertness for the right things, the most important, the most deeply true, things about them?

No law I know of can make us do this, and I doubt whether even God himself can force us to attempt it much less keep us at the effort against our will. But unless the entire witness of our faith is wrong, we must move in the direction of increasing our awareness of other peoples, other religions, and other ways of life if we are to cultivate the growth of worthiness necessary to live in this kind of world at this particular time.

V

Blindness is not a virtue even when practiced by good folk. Blindness is evil especially when practiced as a virtue by Christian folk. Until and unless we can win this profoundly personal battle, we haven't a ghost of a chance to win the victory for a world community.

It is true and it may continue to be true, as one of our playwrights put it, "We live in a time when the truest voices are struck down by the loudest." But let us remember this: the loud voices of hatred, anger, fear, and prejudice are first lifted, not in the marketplace or on the radio or television, but in the sanctuary of our own souls. Once lifted there, they move swiftly into the marketplace, the classroom, and church councils. And once they move in anywhere, they dominate everything else; they narrow our field of awareness, letting us see only what they want us to see, hear only what they want us to hear, and feel only what they want us to feel.

I am all for laws, policies, and institutions that lead toward the control of prejudice, bigotry, and discrimination in every form, but let us not deceive ourselves as to where the first and all-important battle against them must be fought and won: within our own personal, private selves and souls. If we can't win there, we've lost everywhere—and laws and policies aren't worth the paper they are written on. If we can win the battle there, we have a chance to carry the struggle to social levels with power and hope of success.

As we struggle along on the road toward worthiness, we shall need to cultivate the art of being humble about and honest with ourselves, of engaging in candid criticism of motives and deeds.

Here the law of association may help us find out where we are in the scale of awareness. Try a little experiment. If you are a white person, of whom do you first think when you hear the word "Negro"? Some black who may have hurt you, or an ethical giant like Martin Luther King, Jr.?

Or, if you should be a Negro, of whom do you think when the word "white" is used? The members of White Citizens' Councils who defame your life and deny your rights, or the thousands of white educators who have taught in the mission schools of the churches for black people before and since the Civil War and have been an influence of immeasurable good for the elevation of black people?

When we hear the word "Russian" spoken, of whom do we think: Lenin, Stalin, Khrushchev, or the Bolshoi Ballet? All, obviously, are a part of Russia. We cannot think of Russia apart from them, but do we need to think of Russia entirely in terms of the ones we fear?

Here, as elsewhere, humility and honesty suggest the best policy. When we discover that we are simply being dishonest with facts in our attitudes and reactions toward others, we are confronted by a hard choice: either we continue in the exposed procedure of calculated dishonesty, or we strike out in a new direction.

Does not this suggest that we need to extend our lines of personal acquaintance across the lines drawn by our prejudices, fears, and hatreds? This will not be easy. We will do it only as a last resort, but it can be done. As we really get well acquainted with others, we will become more and more alert to the right things about them. We need to know people, not just one or two but many persons, who are on the other side of every chasm that divides the human family into different groups. We simply need to be able and willing to put forth the effort necessary to become acquainted with the things on which we differ as well as those on which we agree. Only as we are willing to do this will we be worthy of the responsibility of the great and grave issues of the day in which we live. This is no time in which to encourage and cultivate parochialism of any kind—not with the world teetering on the edge of annihilation!

I should like to suggest as the culmination of our thrust toward worthiness that we engage in the serious and sustained practice of the worship of God, not only in personal ways but in company with others like ourselves—others who, too, have sinned and come short of the glory of God. Actually, the experience of worship is one of the surest ways to learn how to be honest with ourselves. It helps us as no other experience can, to bring the whole of our life under the judgment of what is ultimately worthwhile. It helps us face the future confident in the reality of a will other than our will, a purpose other than our purpose in terms of which we can find our way. It brings under judgment our little, partisan, and parochial insights by placing them upon the altar dedicated to the God of all men in whose sight all men are precious.

Some such experience as this is necessary if we are to be worthy of the trust of life itself, if we are to be worthy of the greater trust of the shared life, and if we are to be worthy of the greatest trust of all, of losing our life in the service of Almighty God.

12/They Seal Their Loyalty with Their Life

Scripture: *II Corinthians 11:21-30*

I

Legends and traditions to the contrary, we cannot be sure where Paul was buried. There is no reason to question the very early legend that he was executed in Rome, and, assuming that, there is every reason to believe that he was buried there too. Without doubt his friends were given his body for burial, and they must have placed it someplace in or near the city. But we do not know where, and Paul would be the first to insist that that does not matter. What would matter to him should matter in a very special way to us when we renew our pledge of love and loyalty to the church he worked so hard to build.

The heart of his life and faith comes to us time and again in the salutation with which he opens his letters to his people: "Paul, an apostle of Christ Jesus." That was what he lived, labored, and died for—and it is the only adequate description of his life I know. If we wanted an epitaph for him, not to engrave on stone but to wave as a banner in the sky, I suggest this: *"Paul, an apostle of Christ Jesus."* That sets the pattern not only for him but for Christian life and work from that day to our own. It is, therefore, more than a wonderful epitaph for Paul—it is the key which unlocks the door to great loyalty to the Christian church generally and to every local church: we are called to be apostles of Christ Jesus!

Use that key to open the door of our own church, and we shall rejoice in the privilege we have of sharing in her life and work. As we walk through the door we shall see the meaning of and reasons for our greater loyalty to the church. One of the traditional prayers for the church suggests some of these reasons.

> O God, we pray for thy Church, which is set today amid the perplexities of a changing order, and face to face with a great new task. We remember with love the nurture she gave to our spiritual life in its infancy, the tasks she set for our growing strength, the influence of the devoted hearts she gathers, the steadfast power for good she has exerted. When we compare her with all other human institutions, we rejoice, for there is none like her. But when we judge her by the mind of her Master, we bow in pity and contrition. Oh, baptize her afresh in the life-giving spirit of Jesus! . . . Put upon her lips the ancient gospel of her Lord. . . . Fill her with the prophets' scorn of tyranny, and with a Christlike tenderness for the heavy-laden and down-trodden. Bid her cease from seeking her own life, lest she lose it. Make her valiant to give up her life to humanity, that like her crucified Lord she may mount the path of the cross to a higher glory. Amen.[1]

II

Loyalty to the church begins as an act of remembrance. We remember in love "the nurture she gave to our spiritual life in its infancy."

[1] Walter Rauschenbusch, *Prayers of the Social Awakening* (Philadelphia: Pilgrim Press, 1925), pp. 134-35.

Most of us have grown up in the church. Among our earliest recollections are those of going to Sunday school, things—pleasant or unpleasant—that happened there, teachers, picnics, Christmas plays and pageants, and a host of other things.

Who can measure the worth of that kind of influence in the life of a child? While it means more to some than others, the fact of exposure to it is significant for all. We need to grow up in religious thought and life, and the church has helped us do it.

This task of guiding a child toward greater maturity in religion is too great for the church alone, but it is impossible without the church. Family, school, and community have their part to play in the process of maturing, but none of them does the work of the church. This is where we learn to sing the praises of God and Christ, where we learn to read, study, and understand the Bible, where we meet Jesus Christ not only as one who lived in Galilee 1900 years ago but as one who seeks to be Lord of our life, where we learn of the kingdom of God as the pattern after which we should seek to mold our own life and the life of man.

Here in the church is where the meaning of prayer grew to greater maturity, where the petition "Now I lay me down to sleep" was challenged to become "Not my will, but thine be done."

It is a wonderful thing, not only to grow up in the church ourselves but to have the church here for all children—our own and others. One of the most important things we ever say to new people in our community or to our young people as they have their families is, "We want you to bring your children to the church. We'd like to help you help them learn to love God with all their heart, soul, mind, and strength, and their neighbor as themselves."

We remember in love "the tasks she set for our growing strength." When I was no more than six years old, my Sunday school teacher brought us up to sharp attention by asking, "Do you know what God wants you to do?" We were all ears as he said, "Grow in wisdom and strength and in favor with God and man." I had no clear notion of what was involved, but it seemed to involve a long, long time. I recall how sobering it was to step from the public school, attended by children like myself, into the church attended by adults as well as children. The church wasn't "just for kids"; it was for everyone. Even when I only dimly perceived what the preacher was talking about I could tell he was saying something to my parents, teachers, and elders in the town—as well as to me.

And the problems we brought to the church grew up even as we did. The answers that occasioned no question to a ten-year-old mind were pitched battles for the high school and college age. But they occurred in the church. She invited us to grow up religiously, as well as every other way. And she offered to help. It was to her we came for an understanding of marriage and for marriage itself. It was to her we came with our children for their baptism and for their nurture in the faith. It was to her we brought them should death take them from us. In life and in death we found in her the strength we needed step by step of the way.

We remember in love "the influence of the devoted hearts she gathers." I shall never forget an old man, more than half-blind, who was helped into church every Sunday until the day of his death. He did not say it, but he would have understood an elderly hard-of-hearing woman who was a regular attendant at church. A friend asked about her faithfulness, considering her age and deafness, and she said, "That is right; I don't hear much, but I want to show which side I am on."

This sentiment may be prompted partly by fear, but it need not be. Just as she said, some loyalties are so deep-rooted, so meaningful that they demand expression. We just cannot keep them "inside ourselves," they must and will out somehow, somewhere.

The history of a local church is not to be written in terms of building or number of members. Rather, it must be written in terms of "the devoted hearts she gathers" for life and work here.

Week after week several women gather for the "overseas sewing." Once a year more women both create and endure the onslaught of a rummage sale in order to make some money for the church. Other women will work at something else—but pointing toward the same purpose.

A church school is made possible by the earnest cooperation of teachers and parents who fall to the tasks that only they can do—tasks that must be done if we are to have a church school. There is no way we can adequately express our appreciation to the "devoted hearts" who make it possible.

Once a year many men and women will take to the streets to talk to the members about the support of the church. They make their own personal pledges; they are usually active in some organization in the church. They might reason, "Let someone else do this job." Thank God, they do not. The work of the church is theirs to do, and they accept it with joy. Their loyalty to the church is so deep-rooted, so meaningful that they can't keep it inside. This is one way in which they "let it come out," a way in which they "show which side they are on." It is a good thing to be among, to be one of, a group of people whose love for and loyalty to the church moves them to do the work of the church. It ought to challenge every slacker in the ranks to rise up and join them.

We remember in love "the steadfast power for good she has exerted."

There are times when I think that is an overstatement, because the church has wavered all too frequently when she might have moved ahead with confidence. Yet, on the whole, she has been a power for good.

Sometime ago I had occasion to renew and deepen my study of the contribution of religion to the growth of this country. I began with the documents which tell why men left England and the continent of Europe for the wilderness of America. I worked my way through the agonies of the settlement period, through the growth to maturity of the colonies, and finally, to the achievement of independence. It is a stirring story—one without equal anywhere in the world, I think. And at the very heart of the most important moments and movements was the religious motif—the desire to worship God according to the dictates of conscience, the determination to build here a new Jerusalem, no matter what the cost in "blood, toil, tears and sweat," the keen awareness that they were responsible to God for what they were and did. For them, life was an adventure in unending stewardship before God. Such convictions produced much more than the burning of witches by "the lunatic fringe" we so often center attention on; they produced a climate of moral concern and awareness that is an essential part of our heritage. This fact is not lost on some keen observers from other countries. One such said by way of playful criticism, "The trouble with

155

you Americans is you try to be 'moral' about everything."
Then he added, "What a blessed fault!"

The church is concerned, and rightly so, about the moral
climate of society. That is our responsibility and it is our
duty to assume it. We have a right and a spiritual obligation
to try to be "a steadfast power for good" in local elections,
in the shaping of foreign and domestic policies. Short of that
we are no power at all for anything that counts for good.

III

Loyalty to the church involves more than "remembering
in love" these great things. It means consecrating ourselves
in love to certain things that are implicit in our remem-
brances. As the prayer for the church puts it: We must
measure the church by the mind of her Master, Jesus Christ.
We must consecrate ourselves to the task of understanding
more fully what that mind is and where it leads. We must
consecrate ourselves to the task of understanding our own
life and work here in the light of his leadership. We cannot
very well be apostles of Jesus Christ unless we are willing
to do this. There is work to be done in his name and for
the sake of advancing his kingdom—and it is our freely
assumed work. To this end we seek a renewal of faith through
the life-giving spirit of our Lord.

This traditional phraseology sometimes offends or con-
fuses those who are unfamiliar with the New Testament
and the early church. The early Christians were sure that
Christ had actually taken possession of them in their Christian fellowship. Without him they felt weak and helpless;
with him they felt ready for whatever lay ahead—whether
a hard journey or a cross on which to suffer and to die.

When Paul cried, "I can do all things in him who strengthens me," he was saying what everyone felt.

That is what I mean when I say we need to consecrate ourselves to him so completely and sincerely that something of his power and spirit will enter into our thinking and living. We are all in need of that. Such differences in need as exist among us are of degree, not of kind. Only as we keep close to him will we want or try to be his apostles today.

We need to consecrate ourselves to a renewal and deepening of our concern for men and their salvation. The church is a channel through which we can pour our common efforts to preach the gospel to the ends of the earth. We cannot effectively be concerned about men whom we do not honestly love. *Love comes first.* As we love them we will want to help them in the spirit of Christ. Out of love will grow the church where everyone feels needed, wanted, and welcome—feels truly at home.

Which points up the need to be willing to lose ourselves in the life and needs of the world today. No church is an end in itself. It is a means to God's end and aim for this world. The surest way for a church to die is to concentrate on herself and her own needs. The surest way for the Christian spirit to die in each one of us is to think about ourselves, our own pleasure, convenience, and welfare, rather than about what God is trying to do through the church.

One of the great tasks of the church is to keep us aware of the most important and most far-reaching issues which mankind faces. While it is necessary to think about our own life and work, it is appallingly easy to think of little else. But one who is called to be an apostle of Christ Jesus will take the world as his parish for prayer, for thought, and for work.

We are fortunate in the church in so many ways, but none more than these: *We stand* in a tradition of people who have not been content to serve themselves but have either gone out or sent and supported missionaries all over the world; *we stand* in a tradition of fearless social criticism and outlook, not dodging or ignoring the issues of life and death for mankind; *we stand* in a tradition which is committed to the endless task of training our children to love the church and the Christ we seek to serve; *we stand* in a tradition of men and women who have yet to sound the alien note of discouragement, despair and ultimate defeat. It goes without saying that *we stand* in a tradition that will not let us rest—no matter how tired we may think we are.

Mrs. Alben Barkley once wrote of her famous husband, the Vice-President, with wifely pride, "It takes a big man to love something as big as America." That is true—so true. And it takes a much bigger person to love something as great as Jesus Christ and the church that bears his name, the church that aspires to be known as "an apostle of Christ Jesus." We ought to thank God for our opportunity to measure the depth of our appreciation to our fathers before us, and the true extent of our loyalty to Jesus Christ whose name we bear and under whose banner we serve.